Critical Acclaim for
EXPECT A MIRACLE

'Anyone searching for a healthy, loving relationship will find a practical, honest approach in Kathy Freston's *Expect a Miracle*. Her seven simple steps take us deeper into ourselves, in order to attract what we truly desire'
John Gray, author of *Men Are From Mars, Women Are From Venus* and *The Mars and Venus Diet and Exercise Solution*

'A wonderful guide to the search for true love. Kathy Freston writes from the depth of her own knowing, as her faith is obviously based on real experience. She has more than survived, she has triumphed. And you get the feeling reading her book that if she can do it, then so can you'
Marianne Williamson, author of *Everyday Grace*

'Kathy Freston gives sensible, practical advice for advancing spiritually in order to allow love and the right relationship into your life. I can't think of anyone who would not profit from following it'
Andrew Weil, M.D., author of *8 Weeks to Optimum Health*

'In simple and powerful words, *Expect A Miracle* takes the reader on an inspiring journey of love and transformation. Kathy Freston reaches out and touches your heart with her own compelling tale of discovery and revelation'
Barbara De Angelis, author of *Real Moments*

'*Expect A Miracle* is a little miracle of its own: a heartfelt, hands-on guide to transforming your life. Forget The Rules – Kathy Freston shows us the real path to finding a great relationship'
Arianna Huffington, columnist and author of *The Fourth Instinct*

www.booksattransworld.co.uk

EXPECT A MIRACLE

7 Spiritual Steps to Finding the Right Relationship

Kathy Freston

BANTAM BOOKS

LONDON • NEW YORK • TORONTO • SYDNEY • AUCKLAND

EXPECT A MIRACLE
A BANTAM BOOK: 0 553 81615 2

First publication in Great Britain

PRINTING HISTORY
Bantam edition published 2004

1 3 5 7 9 10 8 6 4 2

Set in 11/15.5pt Janson by
Falcon Oast Graphic Art Ltd.

Bantam Books are published by Transworld Publishers,
61–63 Uxbridge Road, London W5 5SA,
a division of The Random House Group Ltd,
in Australia by Random House Australia (Pty) Ltd,
20 Alfred Street, Milsons Point, Sydney, NSW 2061, Australia,
in New Zealand by Random House New Zealand Ltd,
18 Poland Road, Glenfield, Auckland 10, New Zealand
and in South Africa by Random House (Pty) Ltd,
Endulini, 5a Jubilee Road, Parktown 2193, South Africa.

Printed and bound in Great Britain by
Cox & Wyman Ltd, Reading, Berkshire.

Papers used by Transworld Publishers are natural, recyclable products made
from wood grown in sustainable forests. The manufacturing processes conform
to the environmental regulations of the country of origin.

This book is dedicated to my husband,
Tom,
who has given me the gift of his miraculous love.

Contents

Acknowledgments

There are so many beautiful souls to whom I wish to express gratitude for making possible *Expect a Miracle*:

Noah Lukeman, wonderful agent, teacher, and friend, who opened the door for me. Marian Lizzi, my insightful editor at St. Martin's Press, for taking the chance on me and then making it all happen. To Sally Richardson, George Witte, and the wonderful John Murphy and John Karle at St. Martin's, for their energy and enthusiasm. To Caroline Pincus, for expertly sculpting and midwifing the book into fruition. And to Kevin Law, for painstakingly mapping out and being the architect of the writing. To Steve Snider, for his keen artistic vision. Thank you to Judith de Rubini for her expert copyediting. To Kelly Bovino, for her research. To Myra Scheer, Natalie Mines, Madeline Johnson, and Val Brown, for conscientiously promoting Transformational Meditation. To Baret Boisson, for the painting of 'yoga girl' on the cover of the accompanying CDs. To Thom Valentino, for legal advice. To Olivia Rosewood, for her healing presence. To Scott Hobbs, for teaching me to breathe again. To Nancy Napier and Virginia Goldner, for being therapists extraordinaire.

To my parents, Joan and Bill, for allowing me to become exactly the person I am. And to the friends who walked me through my 'dark night of the soul': Julie Branca, Debbi Dion, Mariel Hemingway, Mary Matthews, Nancy McGowan, Maeve Quinlan, Janet Rienstra, Robyn Todd, and Nan Valentino, THANK YOU from the bottom of my heart!

Introduction

When I was a child I always dreamed of meeting my Prince Charming. As a girl raised in this culture I was conditioned to believe that this fantasy man would come in and save me from my lackluster life. He would see me from across the room, we would lock eyes, and that would be *it*. 'Happy Ever After.' So as I came of age I tried ever so hard to find that fantasy man. Many times I even thought I'd found him, my heart swelling with joy, my adrenaline pumping, visions of the future appearing in my mind's eye. But then, invariably, my beloved-of-the-moment would somehow begin to let me down. The relationship would end and I'd be out looking again.

Not only did I date men who were completely wrong for me, but I also tended to go out with guys who somehow drained my energy. Some were just boring, a couple were alcoholic, and one was downright abusive. I kept wanting to see something that just wasn't there and I would try desperately to make right what was wrong. Looking back, I see how empty I felt and how I scrambled to fill my heart with the illusion of love. Like so many women, I was attracted to the idea that I could fix someone and make him see that I was good. Because if someone else saw my worth, most of all Prince Charming, then I surely must be okay.

But no matter how I tried to do whatever it took to find my guy, it always turned out to be a major disappointment. Wasn't there someone out there for me *who would make me feel good*, I wondered?

I went on blind dates and couldn't believe who my friends thought I might like. I tried following The Rules (which, by the way, were recommended to me by my mother *long* before they were turned into a bestselling book), never accepting a Saturday date after Wednesday and not giving *it* up till the twenty-fifth date, and I did get the guy. But the relationship had no honesty or spiritual depth.

I tried going out more, forcing myself to meet 'new types,' but I always came home at the end of the night grateful for my flannel pajamas and the fact that I hadn't married any one of these guys. I even lowered my standards, thinking I'd become too finicky. Still, the results were the same: trying to fit a square peg into a round hole just wasn't working.

Eventually I had to ask myself: Why did I always seem to hook up with men who took me for a ride and left me exhausted? Well, I searched and searched for a reason, a common thread, and what I came up with, ultimately, was *me*. I realized that I was the one allowing these men into my life. I was the common denominator in all these relationships. I was the one who somehow found myself with men who couldn't or wouldn't love me the way I wanted to be loved. There wasn't anything I could do to change the men (God knows I tried), so the only thing left was to change *me*.

I realized that I had to understand *my* contribution in these failed and unfulfilling relationships, and figure out what *I* could do to change the dynamic, so that I might finally meet the right guy for me. And so I took the plunge into deep waters and started working on myself.

I started therapy, joined a Twelve-Step program, and found a spiritual teacher. I began to piece together wisdom from a variety of sources – *A Course in Miracles*, published by the Foundation for Inner Peace, which teaches through lessons and meditations about living in the constant unfoldment of miracles; visualization; meditation; prayer; basic psychotherapy – and then created some new techniques of my own. Eventually these would become my Seven Steps for Transformation.

But first I committed myself to doing personal growth exercises for just twenty minutes, twice a day, and after about twenty days something magnificent happened. I didn't feel desperate anymore, I didn't feel hopeless. In fact, I had an overwhelming sense that something great was on its way. And, lo and behold, guess what happened? I started to attract different kinds of people into my life. Kind. Spiritual. Brilliant. Creative people. And I got more comfortable with the idea that these were the sorts of people I could be with. And that, ultimately, I could actually be married to someone who embodied all that and more.

When I met my husband, it felt like a quiet recognition of something that had just been waiting to happen. There was not the loud boom of fireworks and trumpets, but instead long conversations, laughter, and doing fun things together. Without my *making* anything happen, my heart had finally opened, and in walked Mr Right. Instead of feeling all twisted up and excited inside, I felt comfortable and enlivened. Instead of concentrating on what needed to be fixed in him, I admired him for exactly who he was, and he seemed to bring out my most creative and productive energy. And, finally, instead of always picking at what was wrong, we celebrated this incredible relationship that seemed like a miracle to both of us.

Ever since I began teaching these steps, I have continued to be astonished at their power. I started out just sharing them with friends, then created a series of five voice-guided meditation CDs for Perfect Weight, Finding a Great Relationship, Abundance, Healing, and The Daily Dose (see the ordering information at the back of this book), and finally I opened a private practice to help people manifest their desires. My workshops and classes have been a wonderful laboratory for putting the task of *transforming energy* to work. I have seen an incredible desire and readiness in people to change their lives by changing their very energy. It is the subtle work of meditation, rather than manipulation, that has been and continues to provide miraculous results in the people who go through my Seven Steps of Transformation.

I want to share with you this process that has brought me and so many others to the miracle of being in love, because when you find such a source of bliss, you want to spread it around. You want everyone to feel as good as you do.

In these seven simple steps that you are about to undertake, you will learn to find peace within, to align yourself with the powerful spirit of Grace, and to transform your very energy from that which didn't work into magnificent *magnetism*.

So now that you know my story, let's turn our attention to yours. I figure that if you're reading this book, you have already come to the realization that something is not working with the way you go about getting into relationships. Perhaps you're in one but are looking for a way out; maybe you've been dating but just can't seem to find Mr/Ms Right; maybe you haven't been with a partner in years and have just about given up. But you wouldn't be reading if you'd given up all hope, would you? Perhaps you hear the quiet knocking of your soul seeking deliverance after all.

Relationships are not only precious gifts but also great learning experiences which inspire us to grapple with who we are. The truth is, the miracle of a wonderful partnership awaits each and every one of us, if and when we're ready. But going through the Expect a Miracle process isn't just about attracting the perfect partner. By doing this work you will also become more self-aware and awakened to the world of miracles. That's why I say that this book will not only guide you to finding a great relationship but will also take you on a deeply spiritual journey.

HOW TO USE THIS BOOK

I encourage you to read the book slowly and thoroughly, undertaking all the exercises and meditations. It's not enough to just read *about* something, you have to *participate* in order to experience the true shift in energy. Underline the parts that you want to remember, cut out and tape on to your mirror the prayers and mantras (the sacred invocations that you will find scattered throughout the text) that you want to reuse, fill out the charts with honest answers, and, above all, go into the Expect a Miracle process with an open mind and a joyful heart.

It took a lifetime to create your present situation, so don't expect instant results. I suggest that after finishing the book you go back and use the meditations for thirty consecutive days. Every day of the thirty days, choose one of my mantras and say it as often as you can remember. Mantras are not, as some folks believe, desperate 'affirmations' that we don't really believe but try to beat into our brains anyway; they are statements that *re-mind* us of the truth we already know.

Upon completing each chapter, wait for three days before proceeding to the next step so that the energy of the work settles in. Keep referring back to any particular step that you feel you still have work to do on; there is no 'finish' to our work, it is an ongoing process of lifting and purifying our very energy.

My work is rooted in the belief that we create our own reality, that healthy relationships can occur only when we are ready inside, when we are open to a miracle. Becoming open means trusting and having faith in the benevolence of Grace and realigning ourselves with the power behind it. When that happens, we no longer have to work at finding the perfect relationship, only wait for it to appear. And it will. (By the way, when I use the word *Grace*, I am referring to the spiritual nature of God, an expression of pure and perfect love, which some people call their Higher Power or God Force, Great Spirit, Great Intelligence, or just spirit. Throughout the book please substitute whatever term you are most comfortable with.)

So before we do anything else, I am going to ask you to set yourself up to expect a miracle, to believe that something truly great can and will happen. To believe to your core that it is not selfish to want great love, but simply a loving reception of what our potential is: perfect union. That discovering the love within ourselves and connecting with someone else in a way that breaks through that which is familiar and ordinary is just a part of our life's purpose. You see, that's what a miracle is: a shift from dark to light, from lovelessness to abundant love – a transformation in every sense of the word.

Ready? Let's begin.

EXPECT A MIRACLE

Be Still

You need not leave your room. Remain sitting at your table and listen. You need not even listen, simply wait. You need not even wait, just learn to become quiet, and still, and solitary. The world will freely offer itself to you to be unmasked. It has no choice; it will roll in ecstasy at your feet.

—FRANZ KAFKA

You might think, as so many people do, that to find a great relationship you've got to grit your teeth, go out and make a great effort, and basically do whatever it takes to find the guy or gal. In fact, that might seem easier than what I'm about to propose because you're probably at least familiar with the rules of that game. No, expecting a miracle isn't about *doing* anything. It isn't about changing who you are on the outside. It isn't about getting fit or mastering the art of scintillating conversation or buying a whole new wardrobe.

It's about going deep within and finding out where you are holding yourself back from love. It's about preparing yourself to have the relationship that would fulfill your highest potential. It's about becoming still so that you can listen for cues from your heart and soul, and then just waiting and watching as everything unfolds exactly as it is supposed to. If you can take to heart this one simple idea – that all you need to do is be still and present – everything else, including finding a great relationship, will take care of itself.

In this first step we'll be looking at just how to bring about that sense of inner stillness, so that you are ready for the entry of Mr/Ms Right into your life.

MANTRA

I am breathing and listening. In this stillness I am whole.

It's no wonder we have a hard time getting quiet inside. These days I find that there's almost a macho contest going on about who can work themselves hardest – who can fit more things into their day, survive on less sleep, or afford themselves less vacation time. Hmm, if you win at this game, what's the prize? Maybe you get the worker-bee award for getting the most done, but so what? At the end of the day, have you expressed yourself fully? Have you looked deeply into someone's eyes and known profound love? It's doubtful. When we operate at warp speed, as so many of us do, we go too fast to let the moment illuminate us. I would suggest that this pace is designed by the ego – that part of us that perceives the world as a hostile place, that gets us into power struggles, that keeps us living in fear – to keep us from ourselves and from God.

MANTRA

I rest in sacred stillness, knowing my partner is on the way.

Relationships are the perfect opportunity for growth and high expression, and because growth can be frightening, the best way to keep it away is to stay busy with the dramas of everyday life. Stay bogged down in the energy of simply keeping up and your soul will have no fertile ground for deep love to take root. Sure, life is busy, but it's worth looking at how much of your busy-ness is really necessary and how much is self-created to keep you from the daunting task of growth.

That's why the first step toward expecting a miracle is to become still, to free ourselves from self-created distractions, so that we can hear what's in our hearts and become wide open to love.

The good news is that your life has led you here for a reason. Who you have become is just perfect and ripe for a miracle. And at this point, all you have to do is . . . breathe. Deeply and slowly, breathe. Begin to feel your body, and get in touch with who you are and how you are right now. And with that groundedness, the change can begin.

BASIC GROUNDING MEDITATION

First, let's take the mystery out of meditation: you don't need to do anything radical in order to meditate. Simply find a quiet space that you can call your own while you're meditating. It can be out in nature somewhere, in a church or temple, even in the corner of your bedroom.

If you've never meditated before, I would suggest that you start out lying on your back. That will induce the feeling of relaxation and openness that we're seeking here. Eventually you might want to try the lotus position, where you sit cross-legged with your spine perfectly straight, hands resting on your knees, palms facing up. But in the beginning, it's much more important to get used to being quiet and letting go than it is to force an uncomfortable discipline on yourself. Just start out simply and don't do anything that's painful to your body.

To set the mood, dim the lights, turn off the phone, and light a candle to change the energy of the room. You can also bring in an object that reminds you of your spirituality (such as rosary beads or a crystal) so that the feeling becomes more sacred.

Before you begin, read through the instructions for the meditation so that you don't have to keep interrupting yourself to find the next step. Many people find it helpful to record the instructions in their own voice to that they can just close your eyes and follow along. Remember, this is a personal and private journey, so do whatever you intuit is the right thing for yourself; there are no rules!

Now, let's begin.

Get out a piece of paper and a pen. Find a quiet place to which you can retreat.

1. Lie down.

2. Close your eyes and breathe into your belly.

3. Inhale through your nose, expanding up through the belly, the ribs, and then the chest; then exhale, feeling the breath at the back of your throat as it exits through your nose.

4. Begin to feel the weight of your body, the heaviness of your limbs resting on the ground.

5. Notice the tension buzzing through your nerves and breathe into it with the intention of calming it down.

6. As you breathe, repeat in your mind the word 'now.' As each breath brings you to a quieter place, feel your entire body relaxing.

7. Feel your toes wiggle, feel all the tension release in your ankles, up through your calves, your knees.

8. Let your thighs go limp, feel your hips opening and relaxing.

9. Breathe gently, allowing your belly to expand and release, moving that peace up and through your solar plexus. Then up to your chest.

10. Let your arms flop open and relax.

11. Drop any tension from your shoulders and let all the muscles in your neck go.

12. Stay in this position for a few more minutes, soaking up the feeling of groundedness.

13. Release the tension in your face; your jaw first, then your lips, eyebrows, and scalp. Your entire body is now free and open.

14. Take ten more deep breaths at this point.

15. Then slowly open your eyes, sit up, and take a moment to write a single page quickly and spontaneously about how you feel, without editing at all. Write down how your body feels and any strong thoughts you have.

The grounding meditation is particularly useful for helping you bring about the miracle of partnership because it clears your mind. When we are too 'in our heads,' thinking about our to-do lists and deadlines or rerunning old conversations, we are separated from our Higher Self and might not even notice Mr/Ms Right if he/she were standing right in front of us. When clear and present to the moment, by contrast, we not only attract people to us but can recognize their grace as well.

Mantra

I accept where I am at this moment and allow myself the possibility of change.

The meditation helps us become clear and still, and when we're clear and still power flows in to us as through a vessel, and extends outward. I like to think of it as *being in the Miracle Zone*. Here we experience a heightened sensitivity to ideas and inspiration; problems seem to dissolve or become unimportant, and, above all, we are in touch at the highest level with every living creature.

> To be in the Miracle Zone we have to become attentive to our own internal workings and dynamics, from the higher mind to the body's basic needs and impulses.

It's in the Miracle Zone that we just *know* things, and that we become more of who we are, as if our energy is amped up and projected through a magnificent instrument. And in that 'just knowing' a magical thing happens: we become magnetic to a spiritual and rewarding relationship.

BECOMING MAGNETIC

Becoming magnetic is what this work is all about. It isn't

something you can see or hear; it's just that nameless quality that makes people want to be near you. It's not a matter of beauty or status but more of an inner radiance. Of course, the same can be said of its opposite; no matter how physically perfect we are, if we're not radiating an inner light, we're not really attractive on any deep or lasting level. Can we *become* magnetic? Absolutely.

Magnetism is that which begins as a connectedness within oneself, and then issues forth as a connectedness with others.

In fact, becoming magnetic – by bringing together our body, mind, and spirit in perfect harmony, to a degree that we don't even have to think about it anymore – is the short order for attracting the right partner. As Marianne Williamson says in *A Return to Love*:

Our deepest fear is not that we are inadequate. Our deepest fear is that we are powerful beyond measure. It is our light, not our darkness, that most frightens us. We ask ourselves, who am I to be brilliant, gorgeous, talented and fabulous? Actually, who are you *not* to be? You are a child of God. Your playing small doesn't serve the world. There's nothing enlightened about shrinking so that other people won't feel insecure around you. We were born to make manifest the glory of God that is within us. It's not just in some of us; it's in everyone. And as we let our own light shine, we unconsciously give other people permission to do the same. As we are liberated from our own fear, our presence automatically liberates others.

Of course what we cannot feel toward ourselves cannot be felt by a potential partner. If *we* don't like who we are, why would someone else? This may sound obvious, but so often we are less accepting and less forgiving of our own frailties than we are of anyone else's. Most of us have to work at becoming self-loving.

Now, I'm not suggesting that we can ever get to a place where we always get it right. Life is challenging and we often make mistakes or fall into traps of self-loathing because we know we could have been better. But it is also true that in the process of working through these difficulties we can find forgiveness for our shortcomings and, seeing the innocence and even perfection in ourselves, we can recognize it in another.

To love ourselves is to acknowledge that we are perfect as God created us. That who we are is not a mistake.

In fact, to perceive in such a Graceful way elicits a magnificent and radiant quality. So relax, stop being hard on yourself, accept who you are right now, and begin to open your heart to the possibility that you deserve a miracle.

∞

I met Stephanie when she came to one of my workshops with a goal of learning how to hang on to a guy. I of course pointed out that 'hanging on' isn't exactly an attractive quality, and that maybe there were other issues to deal with.

When she'd met Andrew, a man with whom she might have been a good match, she blew it without knowing exactly how. The truth that came out was that, even though she presented herself in the way she thought would attract him, Andrew said there was something disingenuous and desperate about her, and moved on.

I noticed that Stephanie was visibly uncomfortable in her own skin, not quite inhabiting her body. Even with me, I could see that she was looking for cues on how she should be acting, rather than just being herself. Although she knew she was quite pretty, Stephanie said that men ultimately never wanted to commit to her. She eventually admitted that the more insecure she felt, the more makeup and shorter dresses she wore, but to no avail; everything was a desperate attempt to be liked.

Stephanie did not realize that only by relaxing into her own unique energy and accepting herself would she get the relationship she wanted. She was miserable with herself and hated to be alone, but couldn't understand why no one wanted to commit to her for a lifetime. I told her that the peace and security she sought from a man would surely not come her way when she herself did not have personal and innate knowledge of such qualities. I explained to her that no one wanted to feel like they were the source of someone else's good feeling because, although at first it might be a heady compliment, it would soon become a burden.

Stephanie had no choice but to quietly withdraw into her own energy and make peace with herself. She did this by taking up the rituals of meditation and saying daily mantras. I also coached Stephanie to spend a good month alone, learning to enjoy her own company.

Once she got centered and connected with her Higher Self, she became attractive in a whole new sense of the word. Gone were the short skirts and the desperate measures to lure someone in; Stephanie no longer came from a place of lack (i.e., the fearful ego) but instead radiated magnetism. As a footnote, Stephanie is now engaged to be married to a wonderful man.

The signal that Stephanie was sending was that she was unlikable, even to herself, and hence unattractive to her potential mate in any way other than the superficial. She was resisting the idea that she was, of herself, enough.

Putting on an act in order to gain someone's love is sending a message that who you are is not good enough. There is no self-love in that, and certainly no magnetism. Until we know that we are, of ourselves, enough, we will sabotage anything that comes along indicating otherwise. When we are comfortable with all the aspects of ourselves, self-love and magnetism come naturally.

THE TRINITY SELF

We attract and respond to people at many different levels.

We are three-dimensional creatures, after all, comprised of body (our physical manifestation), mind (our particular personality and identity), and spirit (our unique spiritual path). I call this the Trinity Self. Each element has its own role to play in helping us navigate our lives and connect with other people.

The synergy of the integrated self is what makes us rich and attractive. Without the magic of the spirit, the mind is nothing more than an intellectual machine. And without the rationale and curiosity of the mind, the spirit does not have a vessel through which to express itself. Without the body to contain these ideals, abstracted energies remain ungrounded. Each aspect of ourself influences and enriches the others. We might find a partner we connect with on one level, but still feel unfulfilled because the other two aspects have been asleep.

For instance, we might connect with someone on the 'mind' aspect because we admire their wit and intelligence, but if we aren't in sync with each other's sexual needs or spiritual inclinations, we will eventually become disenchanted and feel unfulfilled. This is not to say one of the two people is in any way to blame, only that the match is not ideal. To settle on someone because he or she connects well with one or even two aspects of ourselves is a compromise that ultimately cheats the soul of full expression. By the same token, we can't expect to find a partner until we have fully awakened each of the aspects within ourselves.

When all parts of the Trinity Self are operating at the

highest level possible, we become powerful magnets for love. Only then do we naturally link up with the partner who can join with us for the lessons and experiences we most need in order to further grow and evolve.

Now, let's get working on becoming magnetic. Remember, this is not about *doing*, it's about aligning ourselves internally so that we are radiant on every level.

Beginning with the Body

Since our first contact with people is by our physical presence, it is essential to start the process of becoming magnetic by being aware of the messages that we are always imparting through our bodies. We are constantly signaling, communicating who we are through our physical being: whether open, attentive, or needy, etc. If we are pent up and tense, we are essentially saying, 'I am too busy – not open for a relationship – go away!' People can almost immediately determine your emotional state by the vibration your body exudes. It goes as far as telling a potentially unhealthy partner where you are weak and can be manipulated, or, on the other hand, someone who might be a good partner, how you can be celebrated and honored.

This idea that our bodies give off vibrations is not just New Age jargon. We are all, fundamentally, energy, and our bodies are expressions of that energy. So in order to be ready to receive love, it's important to know both what our bodies communicate to others and what they are trying to tell *us*. When we say we can 'feel' in our gut that someone is dangerous, that is our body speaking to us. When we have an ache in our heart because we know someone we longed for can't change, or feel a heaviness in our bones when we are grieving, these are important communications to listen to.

The body is a conduit of universal energy, too. Scientific studies have shown that experiences and memories get stored in the nervous system. When we have a profound experience, be it traumatic or illuminating, the body absorbs that energy, the very occurrence of which is being encoded in the cellular memory. It is as if the experience needs a place to reside, needs a place to work itself out within your psyche; so the body stores it in order that the spirit and the mind can access it at their ready. If the experience was too painful to deal with at the time, we repress it, let it sleep, until we are drawn back to healing it in our adult lives.

Interestingly enough, that which has gone emotionally unhealed is usually the first thing that people subliminally respond to. The façade erected by our ego is never hardy enough to fool the intuitive soul.

Because the truth of who we really are is just below the surface, we are always revealing, unbeknownst to us, our issues by acting unconsciously out of the memories stored in our nervous system. Within us is our past, our present, and predictably our future, so in order to shift the potential for our future, we need to thoroughly relax the body and release the trapped fear-based energy.

Mantra

I am grounded and comfortable in my body.

What affects the body on a daily basis? Stress. There is stress from the job, stress from relationships, stress from just getting through the day. And then there are deeper levels of disturbance: old patterns that continue to play out in our lives and gnaw at our sense of well-being. This is not to say we should or can be entirely stress-free, but when we don't appropriately process the tension that results from stress, it infects our whole field of energy, and people pick up on that. Unprocessed stress blocks us from opening up to higher levels of experience.

Think about it. There is nothing less attractive than someone who is tightened up with all sorts of lingering tensions. The same goes for the mind. When the mind is elsewhere, or trying to act out who we think we *should* be, we are not present, not able to connect on any meaningful level. You can't play-act a relaxed state of being; it must be *real*.

But when you access a state of serenity, when you really feel it, how can you help but want more of it? And people can sense the peace in you and they want it too. When you are totally comfortable with yourself and the world, anything can happen!

EXERCISE: SOUND BREATHING

One of the best ways I know to clear deep-seated stress is

with intentional breathing. This next exercise uses the breath to connect you with your emotions and feelings, giving them expression and release through the use of sound.

The exercise takes less than two minutes and can be done anytime you're feeling stressed.

1. Relax and retreat to your quiet space.

2. Sit down with your spine as straight as you can get it, and close your eyes. You are going to take ten long breaths.

3. Inhale, expanding the belly. The deeper you inhale the more extended your belly will get. Shallow breathing does not touch on your emotions. The idea is to go all the way into them with your breath, and pull them out.

4. Take a moment and, without thinking too much about it, find the most prevalent emotion within you. Like the outer layer of the onion, begin with what is most available.

5. Breathe in and experience the emotion as fully as you can, and give it a sound on the exhale, feeling the vibration fill your body as you do. It could be a high, tinny sound of fear or a deep, grumbling sound of frustration: you will find your own voice (not all the emotions have to be negative; we are simply bringing to balance that which has us off).

6. Continue exhaling the emotion with sound while counting on your fingers each breath you take.

7. With each breath peel back the layers of the onion and go deeper into allowing that emotion to be released.

8. Do this ten times with the intention of releasing the body of its tensions and stress, and then open your eyes, giving yourself a moment to acclimate.

We so often take for granted this most healing tool: breathing. Not only does the breath oxygenate the blood, and therefore calm us, but it also raises our electromagnetic field to a higher vibration. When we vibrate at a higher level, we attract the same from others. You will see what I mean after you've done the Sound Breathing exercise for a while. The sounds give your emotional tensions a pathway out, and you'll find that once they're released you operate on a much higher level physically, emotionally, and spiritually. Your body is a vessel through which Grace flows. The clearer you are, the more radiant and magnetic you become.

∞

Melissa came to me because, as she quoted a Twelve-Step slogan, she was sick and tired of being sick and tired. She'd been through a lot of relationships that ended badly. They all had different reasons for going sour, but the toll they took was that each one added to Melissa's stress and the physical manifestation of it: she walked around looking like a victim waiting to be hurt again. She had slumped shoulders as if she were carrying around suitcases full of lead bricks, each one bearing the name of a man who rejected her.

Because Melissa believed that there must have been something essentially wrong with her, the men she dated ended up confirming that belief. It was no wonder that she was unable to find anyone with whom she could share life's joys and challenges. It was as if she were moping around, expecting the next failure to confirm her disposition yet again. Mighty attractive!

After I suggested Melissa begin taking dance classes, she learned how her body conveyed a story. With each move, she learned that her spirit followed what her body postured. For example, when her chest expanded as she danced, she felt a release of her spirit, as if something opened up inside of her. Melissa actually felt as proud and confident as her posture indicated.

Beforehand Melissa had been unaware that her body was holding her hostage by refusing to let go of a lot of resentment and self-loathing. She was, unbeknownst to her, an advertisement for a doomed relationship. Melissa had, up until this point, attracted relationships that would, in the end, leave her feeling rejected and justified in her hopelessness.

Once she began to get in touch with her body, learning the art of physical awareness, Melissa became someone who not only carried herself more beautifully, but also sent a completely different signal about what she had to offer and expected from a partner.

Melissa is a perfect example of how the body can demonstrate when the Trinity Self is out of balance. In order to evolve her relationship situation, she began by changing her awareness of how she held her body. Through the art of dance Melissa reconnected with the uniqueness of her spirit. She had grown so accustomed to the idea that she was not enough and wasn't destined for love that she kept manifesting disappointment and failure. Melissa had forgotten how to express openness for so long that she became her own self-fulfilling prophecy. But because Melissa took action to open up, the Trinity Self was able to lift from disharmony and become more powerful.

Opening the Mind

When magnetizing a new relationship, it is just as important to keep an open mind and a sense of joyful anticipation as it is to feel really good in your body. If we are willing to see things differently, they have a way of *showing up* differently.

When our minds are open, there are no walls or barriers to curb the flow of energy and everything becomes possible. Just as a brilliant painter allows his subject to flow from inspiration through his hands and onto the canvas, so can we allow Grace to guide us to great and undiscovered love in our lives. But that can only happen when we have a clear slate and say to ourselves: 'Okay! I really don't know what this is going to look like, but I sense that something beautiful is coming.'

Think of how refreshing it is to meet someone who doesn't have a preconceived idea of who you are; you shine as your best self. When someone is free to assume great things about us (and that's something you can just *feel*) we tend to become that greater part of ourselves.

On the other hand, when we come from a place of limited thinking, we project that limitation onto potential partners. *A Course in Miracles* says '. . . a thought never leaves its source.' So to judge someone comes from and continues to create self-loathing. That's not to say you can't choose not to be with someone, but rather suggests that we say 'no' out of love, not judgment. If we unconsciously expect someone to treat us a certain way or prove yet again to be a disappointment, guess what, we'll get to be right.

But does being right make us happy? No. Does being right put us in a fulfilling relationship? No. Being right only means we have succeeded in perpetuating an old paradigm of unfulfilling relationships. Having negative expectations in our minds is like putting up a wall that keeps love away.

Of course it's hard not to succumb to cynicism when it comes to relationships, and even about who we ourselves are as partners. We see things happening over and over in our lives and finally begin to expect them. But if we do not shift out of this expect-the-worst mentality, the world will continue to deliver us our worst fears. If we believe that all men cheat, what we will find is that the men we come across do, in fact, cheat. If we believe that women are always looking for the bigger, better deal, then the type of women we meet up with will prove us right.

Sometimes we are *forced*, by illness or trauma or some other life-altering experience, to open our minds. But we don't have to wait for disaster to strike. We can choose to change our patterns in gentle recognition of the truth – that we are beautiful expressions of God's love and that our highest potential is that we are deeply loving and loved. I personally favor the latter option.

Mantra

My mind is open to divine inspiration.

Indeed, to expect a miracle requires that we forgo the cynicism and pessimism about relationships that many of us have spent a lifetime cultivating. I'm not suggesting that our pessimism was not created out of valid experiences. In fact, I believe that the experiences we've had are extremely valuable because when the miracle comes we are able to truly embrace it, having completely transcended our suffering.

To break out of the self-fulfilling cycle of cynicism and negative expectation, we must open our minds by lifting the judgments that bar the miracle from manifesting. So, now that we have learned to honor our body and esteem it with relaxation, we can begin to open our mind to a miracle.

Discovery consists not in seeking new landscapes, but in having new eyes.

—MARCEL PROUST

Paul Bowles wrote in *The Sheltering Sky* of the invisible veil that protects us from sensing and experiencing all that there is. It protects us, this veil, but it also keeps us in the dark.

Mantra

I open myself to the great and magnificent energy, which is constantly awaiting my invitation.

The object of the next exercise is to help you pierce the veil so that you can begin to recognize your judgments and open up to new ideas about who is right for you.

WRITING EXERCISE: THREE STAGES TO OPENNESS

In this exercise you will be looking closely at your own judgments and attitudes – both obvious obstacles to an open mind. You will be using writing to help bring your thoughts and feelings out of the realm of the ephemeral and into clear view.

1. Get present with where you are now. Take the next minute and write, without censoring, what the feelings are in your body. Allow whatever comes up to come through your fingers onto the paper. Even if it doesn't

make sense, write it all down. Time yourself so that you are busy for one full minute in each of these stages.

2. Think about any lingering judgments you have about yourself or someone you may have been interested in. Notice where you can't see beyond the initial veil of that judgment to the potential underneath. Write in a stream of consciousness every feeling that comes up and expand how it affects your ability to give and receive love.

3. Now make a conscious decision to lift these assumptions. What would you see just below the surface? How would things unfold differently if you came from an open mind?

A miracle is a shift in consciousness, a jump to a higher level, and it only takes a split second for this to occur. Somewhere in us, though, we have to make the decision to change our energy on a core level. Change the energy and the experiences change. For instance, once we learn to see through the eyes of our higher selves, we come from a loving place rather than a fearful one. With that, problems are magically transcended and people just show up differently. Because we are not limited by our fear, our relationships are not dictated by our old negative assumptions. We become fertile ground for the miracle of love to take root.

For one human being to love another: that is perhaps the most difficult of all our tasks, the ultimate, the last test and proof, the work for which all other work is but a preparation.

—RAINER MARIA RILKE

The journey to finding a perfect partner is an expansive one. It's not only about manifesting the relationship, but also transforming the inner mechanisms that had, to date, kept us from meeting that special person. We become the sort of individual we'd always hoped existed.

In finding our own power we realize that, in fact, there is not so much to do on an external level, but rather we only need access our inner magnetism. Instead of striving and contriving to find someone out there, we simply need to be present. This beautiful presence, which is born of our radiant stillness, is the most attractive quality we could embody. It takes work to be quiet, to do nothing, and allow the miracle to unfold. This posture goes against everything we've been taught in western culture, and unlearning it requires patience.

Most people will never endeavor this transformation; it is often uncomfortable and confrontational, but the rewards are astounding. No one starts out being perfectly open and available for a spiritual match; it takes commitment, faith, and joyful expectation. Miracles are always coming toward us, more abundantly than you could ever imagine. It is simply a matter of being open and ready to receive them. Our stillness is the ideal ground in which to plant that seed of perfect partnership.

In this chapter you've learned to relax your body and open your mind; you've worked on becoming more magnetic by awakening body and mind, two of the three parts of the Trinity Self. In the next chapter, we will begin the journey to awaken you (or awaken you further) to spirit. Here is a prayer I use to ready myself for that journey:

Prayer for Stillness

Grace, surround me with Your light, infuse me with Your love so that I might know the perfect peace of being still. Quiet my mind of all the chatter, fill my heart with recognition of Your presence.

And guide me into the deepest regions of Your temple. Where I am scattered, hold me together, and where I am fearful, show me Your truth. In this stillness, let me be a vessel for Your love.

Amen

Here are some tips to help you make the practice of stillness a part of your every day.

Seven Everyday Tips to Assist in Step 1, Being Still:

1. Begin each day with a prayer that gets the energy open and flowing.

2. When you begin to feel anxious and stressed, close your eyes, breathe deeply, and count down from ten backwards.

3. Identify great qualities in people when you meet them. Give them a chance to *have* great qualities.

4. Look in the mirror and see where your face is holding tension. Relax the muscles, and with that, relax the stress that goes along with it.

5. When you meet someone new, suspend judgment, and note how you feel about yourself.

6. Think of how you've created miracles for someone else: it's a great way to make one possible for yourself as it opens up the flow.

7. Wake up thirty minutes earlier than you usually do and partake of a spiritual ritual.

Invite Grace In

> *Remembering is like knowingness that wells up inside you. Call for that knowingness, find it, and pay attention to it, and it will tell you clearly what you want to know. Call for that knowingness, and it will allow you to feel loved beyond imagination, eradicating pain, loneliness, and unworthiness. Set your doubts aside as to whatever that knowingness within may be; it's as real as you are, because it's what you are.*
>
> —Lynn Grabhorn, *Beyond the Twelve Steps*

∞

Now that you have begun to move into an inner stillness, to relax your body and open your mind, it is time to welcome spirit and the beneficent force in the universe, Grace, into the arena of your future relationship.

In every moment we choose to come from fear or love.

In order to get to the place where we are always choosing love, we have to learn to surrender our tenacious will and, through prayer and meditation, ask the spirit of Grace to help us.

Relationships are the intangible expression of the soul's deepest longing; we are ephemeral beings and in order that we might find ourselves in that perfect partnership, we must access the part of ourselves that is spirit. It's not a matter of acting one way or the other, but of becoming men or women who channel the energy of graceful attraction. Being in a soulful relationship is the penultimate way to find and express that message.

In this step I am going to help you develop your spiritual practice, so that a soulful union becomes inevitable, as it is the law of spiritual evolution for love to expand itself.

The Art of Surrendering

It can be hard to admit that you are not yet where you want to be in terms of a relationship. That perhaps the way you have gone about things hasn't brought forth the best results. But at some point in our lives most of us come to see that despite our considerable efforts we aren't getting what we want, that we are powerless in some manner and have to consider doing things differently.

It can be pretty discomfiting to surrender like this because we think we are in control of our lives and that it will all just grind down to nothing if we stop policing things. But that's not the case at all. Surrendering allows you to relax into the knowledge that there is a greater intelligence at work in the universe and that you don't have to be on red-alert at all times.

When I was a child, I used to have a recurring nightmare about getting behind the wheel of a big Chevy and trying to drive. I must have been about four feet tall and couldn't quite see over the dashboard. The car would lurch forward and I would squeeze the steering wheel and hang on for dear life as the car careened out of control until I finally woke up. That's what it's like in our lives now when we think we need to be in complete control without having the ability to do so. It's impossible, we're not big enough, not mature enough to handle everything; we're not even meant to. It may feel humiliating at first, to admit how we've screwed things up, but in the end it's a relief to move aside and let someone else drive.

In our powerlessness we find our greatest strength.

Once we recognize that what we're doing is ineffective, it only makes sense that we would make a conscious choice to do things differently. By admitting that perhaps there is a force greater than ourselves that has something better in mind for us, and knows how to get it done, we can then relax, let go of the pressure that clouds us, and become clear and radiant. And, yes, magnetic.

That's what surrender is all about. Letting go of your

small-minded plan and allowing spirit's Grand Plan to unfold. This does not mean admitting defeat or failure but simply conceding that you don't always know what or how to do everything, that you are not all-powerful. Maybe what, or who you would have settled on, isn't half the relationship you *could* have had, had you been patient and let the Universal Mind work its magic. Just think about it: If God could create this universe, He can certainly work out your relationship.

Marianne Williamson always tells this story which, to me, sums it up perfectly. '. . . Say you're at a train station and this train pulls in, and since you've been waiting a long time, you try jumping in without paying too much attention. The door starts closing on you and you're screaming to the conductor to let you in. He tells you to get off, and that it's not the train you want; but you *insist* and force yourself in because you're sick and tired of waiting and it's cold and you're pretty darn sure that this is the train you want. The conductor gives up because you've created such a stir that now you're holding up traffic. He pulls away with you inside. And what pulls up in back of it, now that the traffic has cleared? Your train. But you're off on a trip heading somewhere else because you wanted to do it *your way*.' Sometimes our impatience and insistent will to do things our own way doesn't get us where we need to go. Sometimes we have to step aside and assume that our 'train' is coming. By just ceasing the *act of trying*, things begin to show up differently, and we find any mistrust we might have about trying to find a partner naturally melting away.

* * *

So how do you begin to surrender? As with anything else, you first have to become conscious of what you're doing. And so you begin by noticing how you feel when you are trying to manipulate, by feeling the tightness in your body when you try to control a situation that isn't within your control. Once aware of your ineffective behavior, you simply take a deep breath, close your eyes, and say 'Thy will be done.' And then let it go. This is the most powerful prayer you can make because you are agreeing to step aside in order that the highest possible thing might happen. It's not about giving up and going home, but rather moving over and inviting the benevolent energy of God's will – Grace – to take control.

Mantra

> *I surrender my thoughts of how things should be, and allow Grace to show my good to me.*

We're entering unfamiliar territory here and I know it can be *frightening*. We all want so much to know when change will happen or what it will look like, but we can't. When we were kids sitting in the backseat of the car, asking if we were there yet every five minutes, our parents knew that we were well on the way to reaching our destination, but since we didn't have firsthand knowledge of the journey, we were skeptical. The same goes for us now in the realm of finding a great relationship: it's hard to trust that things will unfold perfectly for us if we can't see *how* they're going to unfold. But if what you've been doing hasn't been working, isn't it worth trying to surrender, to relax and assume that the Universal Mind is at work, making it all come together for you?

I guarantee you, once you get your desperate hold on things out of the way, everything *will* come your way. As they say in AA, 'Let go and let God.' The great paradox here is that the less we get involved in trying to make a relationship happen, the better able we are to allow one to enter.

SURRENDERING JUDGMENT ABOUT WHO'S RIGHT FOR US

Of course in all this talk of surrendering, there are still a few things we *can* control, one of the most important ones being deciding *how* we're going to perceive a situation or person. We can choose to see them through the filter of our own fragile sense of self-worth or we can see the possibility of the quiet perfection that exists in all things. I'm not saying you have to agree to date the guy with the lampshade on his head, only that we can only really see each other if we approach everyone without judgment. When you pre-judge people, you erect a wall through which a potential partner cannot even be seen. Look for faults and that's all you'll see. See the perfection in your fellow human and perfection will appear before you.

When we take it upon ourselves to decide who is good or bad or right or wrong, we close ourselves into a very small box. Choosing from an open heart not to be with someone is entirely different from turning up your nose and diminishing someone. Having an open heart doesn't mean you can't make value judgments and lovingly say 'No, thank you,' but that you don't automatically assume a lack.

Another thing we *can* control is where we put our energy and focus our attention, be it on obsession with what we don't yet have or enriching ourselves spiritually. And, lastly, we control the choices that we make in how we communicate with people and how we show up in our lives everyday. The kind of person that we want to meet won't materialize (or certainly wouldn't call us if they did!) if we are not embodying the very same loving qualities that we seek.

Of course the idea that we were ever in control in the first place is an illusion. If the six billion or so people on earth each thought they had supreme power over their lives, imagine the chaos we'd be in. This is not to say that the world has not been in a dark place; this century has been the bloodiest yet. But if you look around there is a quiet revolution going on; people are embracing their spirituality now more than ever. And that spirituality does not just dictate our morality, or even politics, but every aspect of our lives, including relationships.

Let's take a look at some of the things we can change and some that we can't. Once you see what you are not able to control, try to surrender the urge.

YOU CAN'T CONTROL	YOU CAN CONTROL
Anyone else	What you do with your day
The outcome	How you take care of your body
Someone else's opinion of you	Your self opinion
Society at large	Who you invite into your life
Your feelings and moods	Your thoughts
Addictions	Your need to control
Nature	Home environment
God	Your character
Fate	Karma and Dharma

Universal Mind, which is pulling all the strings all the time in order that we might self-actualize, wants us, in fact, to surrender in order that a higher good be done.

Once you can completely accept where you are presently, a particularly painful situation no longer needs to attach itself to you, trying ever so vigilantly to shake loose your grip. Accept, and then surrender. Then the energy clears, the process of magnetism works its magic, and there is space for new energy to enter.

THE MYSTICAL MIND

In her book *Enchanted Love*, Marianne Williamson talks about a Mystical Third, a presence that is invited into a relationship between two people that they might not just be the couple in love but a vessel through which Grace is expressed. The harmony of the two who have found each other resonates in such a way that you can just *feel* the presence of God. For them to surrender their relationship to Grace does not take away from what they have, but adds to it with the essence of the Mystical Third.

Again, surrender means recognizing that we cannot control other people or situations. It also means letting go of the past so that it doesn't torment us, and in turn we are freed of any limited idea of what the future will bring. Relationships happen when we stop trying to make them happen. It doesn't mean you stop caring, it just means you give up the desperation.

I have always found the Serenity Prayer particularly comforting in times of anxiety:

Serenity Prayer

God, grant me the serenity to accept the things I cannot change, the courage to change the things I can, and the wisdom to know the difference.

Brilliant in its simplicity, this Twelve-Step prayer is truly a lifesaver when we're bogged down with fear and on edge with trying to figure it all out.

∞

Candice was in a relationship with a highly successful lawyer. When it started out he lavished attention onto her, was highly complimentary, predicting great things for their future. As the relationship progressed Candice began to notice William drank a lot, and that when he drank, he got mean. William was someone who constantly needed assurance that he was loved and desired. No matter how much Candice told him that she'd do anything for him to prove her love, and that he was the greatest thing that ever happened, William just seemed to pull further away by acting out sexually with other women and ignoring her. She tried so desperately to change him; brought him to church, therapy, Twelve-Step meetings. She even compromised herself by doing sexual acts she thought would bring him back. But nothing was ever enough.

Candice wanted to return him back to the man she had thought he was, but it never seemed to happen. Instead of moving on like her friends urged, she stayed, trying to control William and his behavior.

When I met Candice I saw the perfect candidate for Al-Anon. We worked together on learning to surrender and she started going to daily meetings. In Al-Anon, Candice learned that nothing you do can change the addict because it's the addict who needs to make that decision. So she was left with the choice: to hang in there or to leave. But Candice kept remembering how great it was in the beginning and how she had hoped that William was her Prince Charming. As much as she didn't want to let go of him and the dream that she had for them, Candice knew that she had to surrender the situation to God and let herself be guided as to which way to go.

With increasing regularity Candice would repeat to herself 'Thy will be done'; she would say it under her breath or silently to herself. Even in the middle of conversations with William, she kept consciously pulling her will out of the situation and turning it over to God. Gradually she felt less attached to him and saw clearly how William was not the illusion he presented in the beginning. Her need to change him into what she wanted him to be diminished and she left him without much fanfare.

Although Candice went through a period of feeling empty and sad, her continued surrender delivered her into a peaceful assurance that she was under God's care and would be provided for. Sure enough she met her future husband on a blind date and to this day is grateful for her trial by fire in learning to invite Grace into her life.

The thing about surrender is that when we don't do it voluntarily, life will progressively nudge (or sometimes just all-out shove) us toward embracing it anyway. Disease, trauma, natural disaster, and even our own obsessive dramas – something will come along and force us to our knees so that we have no choice but to move aside and let a greater force take over. Indeed, it is often by exhaustion that we come to grips with how we've been hanging on to and micromanaging every detail of our lives. Alcoholics use the phrase 'bottoming out' to describe how bad it needed to get before they said, 'No more, I give up.'

Surely we don't need to 'bottom out' in such painful ways to recognize how important it is to surrender. We can embrace the miracle of being taken care of by the simple recognition that Good Will is *intended* for us. The very meaning of Grace is 'the influence or spirit of God operating in humans to regenerate or strengthen them.' Notice the positive intention inherent in the concept. We are not being reprimanded, but cared for and spared the illusion of control. Surrender, acceptance – this conscious letting go returns us to stillness, and it is in that stillness that we tap into Grace, the source of all miracles.

UNDERSTANDING GRACE

Perhaps you're still having a hard time wrapping yourself around the idea of a miracle. According to *A Course in Miracles*, 'a miracle is a radical shift in consciousness from a thought process based on fear to a thought process based on love.' Note the part that says 'shift in consciousness.' What this great teaching is telling us is that it's *all in our head!* In other words, we can change our reality by changing our thinking.

What does this really mean? That if we shift into a greater consciousness, one of love, we can tap into God Force. And if that force can move mountains, it can certainly find you a relationship. To come from love, then, is to operate on a plane where physical laws don't mean a thing, where time and space don't exist and things can materialize in an instant. The Course calls this 'the holy instant.'

> *Each friend represents a world in us, a world possibly not born until they arrive, and it is only by the meeting that a new world is born.*
>
> ANAÏS NIN

Even Webster's Dictionary corroborates this view of a miracle, defining the word as 'an event or action that apparently contradicts known scientific laws and is hence thought to be due to supernatural causes, especially to an act of God.' Throughout history there has been ample evidence of the miraculous – everything from a woman becoming pregnant when the doctor said there was no chance to sudden fortune coming at the eleventh hour of debt. At the time, these miracles astounded those who witnessed them, but later they seemed to have been something just waiting to happen. It's important to grasp this because once you do, once you recognize that life can change in an instant, you can relax into a steady state of joyful expectation.

Miracles can come in many forms and through so many different experiences. The fact that the body continues to heal itself day by day, that alcoholics can find sobriety, or that a parent might find near-superhuman strength to save their child in a car accident, are all proof of this. But miracles can also find their way to us through illness or after hardship because it is in that state of desperation that we turn our hearts over to God and plead for Grace. Miracles also materialize for us when a powerful person is praying or meditating on our behalf.

If we don't actively invite in the miracle, we are often forced to our knees by any means possible for healing. But here we want to make the process more conscious. We want to do the inviting, to learn to manifest the miracle of finding a partner in ways we can actively choose and participate in. To do this is a matter of shifting energy from within and then projecting it out into the world differently. This is quite a task, and we need assistance and guidance to undertake this transformation. It is at this point that we are best off turning to Grace.

To invite in Grace, the first thing we have to do is figure out what's holding us back and dismantle those blocks. We have to redesign our thought patterns, perceptions, and actions. We have to open up the flow of energy that is untapped. But most importantly, we have to desire *transformation* from the deepest reaches of our soul. That's the rule: 'Ask and you shall receive.'

Now this doesn't mean that you can just snap your fingers and get exactly what it is you had in mind. What it means, instead, is that if you are open and willing to have a deep change occur in your Trinity Self, the internal mechanism that navigates your life *will* change course. Whether we know it or not, we get what we expect. The universal mirror simply reflects back to us what, on the deepest level, we believe is coming our way. And we never get more than we are ready for. It's true. Change will happen as quickly or as slowly as you can handle.

Mantra

Miracles are my constant potential and I now open myself to their manifesting.

To expect a miracle is to believe that we are all in God's care, that we are potential mediums of an energy that is constantly making its way toward human enlightenment.

There is no way to logically describe what happens as a miracle unfolds, only that it breaks down all barriers, melts all defenses, and defies the physical laws of this world.

Occasionally in life there are those moments of
unutterable fulfillment which cannot be completely
explained by those symbols called words. Their mean-
ings can only be articulated by the inaudible language
of the heart.

—MARTIN LUTHER KING, JR.

If you consider some of the great events in history, you
can witness the hand of Grace at work. Look at the effect
Gandhi had over a country that knew only oppression and
warfare. He found a nonviolent approach to a problem that
seemingly knew no other answer. When nothing seemed
possible, the willingness of this man to believe that something transcendent could happen, something beyond
human comprehension could blast his people from one
reality to another and set them free, was crucial. His actions
and faith gave way to a profound change that still re-
verberates in our times.

Consider the discovery of penicillin being a complete
'accident.' When Alexander Fleming was studying
staphylococci he noticed that the germ grew less intensely
where it sat in a dish nearer some mold. Growing more of
the mold that came to be called penicillin, he was to discover, seemingly by chance, the first of a whole new type of
medicine – antibiotics. This 'miracle' has saved millions of
lives since.

The crucial point here, though, is that Gandhi and
Fleming were in a state of expectation when the 'transcendent event' happened. They made themselves available

to the miracle of possibility, but also conscientiously set out to be facilitators of that change. They set their will to do something and then held to the notion that a miracle was on the way, thus becoming conductors of a great force of transformation.

These are miracles that boggle the mind when you think about the scale of their largesse. It is something people will talk about for many years and many books have been written about the mystery that surrounded them.

But there is no qualification, no order of importance when it comes to a miracle. We can attract the miracle of a fulfilling relationship just as surely as Ben Franklin invented the lightning rod to conduct electricity. It wasn't possible the moment before he discovered the vessel, but in that instant the world became illuminated. Ever present within us is the potential for a significant shift from darkness to light.

At the same time, if we are not willing, for whatever reason, the miracle will likely remain blocked. Remember that because we are all connected in the spirit realm, your good is everyone's good fortune. So consider seriously that your imminent relationship is for the good of everybody and is in fact a gift not only for you, but also for the entire universe. By your willingness to receive love into your life, you are opening the door for everyone involved and connected to you to experience a higher level of love. The willingness is up to you.

Make no mistake. Willingness is the key. When our

energy becomes infused with intention, it creates a new paradigm, lays the groundwork for having a partnership. It's similar to setting up the architecture of a computer program: once the basic infrastructure and connections are created, and the right questions are asked so that information can be organized, everything thereafter falls into its allotted system. Set the architecture up and the details will fill in naturally.

Perhaps you are saying to yourself: of course I am ready and willing, but it hasn't happened yet! Let's consider what has to happen in order for this transcendence to occur: you have to shed the old, comfortable skin. You literally have to re-create yourself. Sometimes we cling to our habitual life because we can make sense of things that way, we know how to act, who we are, and what to expect. But when we are able to raise our vibration by aligning ourselves with the universal power of Grace, we invite the love we deserve.

∞

When I met Sally she was completely convinced that all men cheated. No matter what anyone said, her experience from her father, followed by her own dating, told her that eventually a man would give in to boredom or hormonal need and another woman would displace her.

A technique I used with Sally is something I call Evidence of the Other. We sat down and made a list of men that she knew and respected who did not cheat. When she stumbled, I helped her add to it historical couples who have been loving and monogamous as well. And of course they did exist; it's just that she had never focused attention on those guys before because they didn't confirm her already deep-seated beliefs.

When we did the exercises, I literally saw a shift in her energy: her eyes lit up, the muscles in her face lifted, and I could see something inside Sally opening. She no longer held to her assumption that all men cheated. And then, of course, the behavior of the men she drew to her was different. Sally had been emotionally attuned to cheating men, so that's whom she'd attracted and hooked into. By finding evidence that her belief system was not ironclad, Sally cracked open the door for a miracle and began meeting men with values that aligned more closely with her own needs.

We'll go into this further in Chapter 4 when we work on dismantling old belief systems, but for now try the following exercise. Sit down now and set out, almost like a lawyer, to find evidence that disproves your outmoded belief system.

EXERCISE: EVIDENCE OF THE OTHER

1. Take twenty minutes and find evidence that supports the idea that things can change in an instant. Remember situations in your life that seemed unworkable and note how they just seemed to work out perfectly in the end.

2. Then explore in friends or acquaintances, or even in literature, stories of how people found each other against all odds.

3. Lastly, find what you have in common with them, see how you relate to them, and intellectually connect to their success.

Your Belief As It Is	Evidence of the Other	What We Have in Common
Example: All men cheat	Example: Mary and Joe Smith have a loving, monogamous relationship . . .	Mary is no smarter or prettier than I, and we are both from the same background and I am just as likely to meet someone like Joe.
Example: Nice guys finish last	Example: Tom Hanks won the Academy Award and he is married to the beautiful Rita Wilson . . .	Tom Hanks seems to be a kind and down-to-earth guy, just like I am.

There, now do you see? If it can happen to someone else, it really *can* happen to you. We are all connected, and no one is more or less deserving of a miracle. So breathe in the idea that, with the Divine Hand at work, everything is about to change. And so it is.

PRAYER AND MEDITATION

The practices of prayer and meditation are the most direct ways to initiate manifesting a relationship. They bring us clarity about what we really want, and nothing comes to us unless our intentions are clear. Many people think of prayer as arrogant, as if we think we can tell God what to do. But that's not the way I see it at all. Prayer is not a short order for God to run out and fill for us, but instead a quiet link in communication that we might know what we have to do in order to have what we seek. Prayer and meditation is quite simply, communion with God. What possibly can't happen in such a sacred space?

When we enter the mystical realms of the spirit, all the disillusion of lovelessness melts away and only the essence of truth remains: that love has always been right there in front of us, just awaiting our readiness. When we are in that Miracle Zone, we know who we are, what we have to do, and that all is already ours.

Prayer is not wishful thinking. It is not a weak plea for something we cannot do for ourselves. It is, in fact, the undertaking of the co-creation of our lives. When we pray, we are stating that we, of ourselves, can do nothing great and meaningful without honoring the holy guide within who leads us to our highest path.

> *There must be the generating force of Love behind every effort destined to be successful.*
>
> —HENRY DAVID THOREAU

So let's talk about what it is to pray. So many people have a lot of judgment or fear around the idea of prayer, thinking that it means they have to lead a puritanical lifestyle complete with taboos and rules, but this is not at all the case. Grace only wants us in conscious contact so that our lives may be used for the highest of purposes. Again, that is to express and manifest love. So, to be in communion, you want to feel, in every cell of your body, a sense of fusing with the Holy Spirit. It's as if you invite the Divine into your being, and every single bit of you is enlightened by that presence. Through the act of prayer, you *become* more Grace-full: radiant, loving, and magnetic.

Mantra

> *I am in constant communion with God in every action I take.*

Because prayer emphasizes faith, it takes away our struggle and the lower, cloying energy of the ego. Faith implies a state of confidence and expectation, and in order to have a miracle the posture of quiet knowingness is necessary. When you send a clear signal for what you want, it cannot help but to appear in a time and form that is comfortable for you and in alignment with everyone else's good.

Also, when praying, it is best to ask only for something that is for the good of everyone involved. For instance, praying for John Doe to leave his wife and come to you not only diminishes what *could* happen, it also holds the potential for hurting someone else. Such a request is not aligned with the energy of Grace. To cling to such a prayer only freezes the forward momentum of the prayer's outcome.

A common glitch that sometimes stops us is that we feel guilty because, on a deep level, we don't think we deserve God's attention. For some reason, we have not forgiven ourselves or don't think we've done enough to deserve a miracle. But, once again, there's no order of priority or scope when it comes to miracles; everything is possible, all the time, for *everyone*. Our sense of guilt can be assuaged first by giving thanks for what we already have, and then asking forgiveness for our shortcomings. Do you think God expects us to be perfect before we come to Him? Of course not; if He did, He'd be waiting an awfully long time, just like the Maytag repairman – tapping his fingers, waiting and waiting.

Prayer is a very personal process. You don't have to adhere to any particular formula, tone, or dogma. Your intention of communion is all that is necessary. That said, here's a simple beginning you may want to explore.

How to Pray

When you can get a moment of privacy, sit down and close your eyes. I've found it particularly helpful to hold an image of what God is to me in my mind. By doing this your subconscious clearly gets the message that you're accessing something other than itself. Your whole body responds to the feeling of transcending what has been within your reach up to this point. What you see will be entirely up to you. God may appear to you as an angelic figure swathed in white robes, or a Buddha, or a beautiful glowing white light without form. Whatever the image, let it be a pure source of light and love. Focus your attention on the image up into the center of your forehead, into what the Eastern cultures call the Third Eye, and see yourself communicating with this divine energy. Actually visualize a field of energy circulating between you and God.

When I pray I begin by recognizing that this communion is a gift to me for which I'm thankful. I thank God for all the good that's already in my life, the things I am so appreciative of, and then I proceed to ask for guidance in a particular situation. In seeking a relationship, I would ask that I be shown what I need to do or understand so that I might find the great partner who I know is out there waiting for me. Then I sit quietly and allow any inspiration to become clear before I ask release from the patterns that have held me back. I humbly ask that God remove whatever it is I've been doing out of fear. In my mind's eye, I see the flow of energy between the God image and myself intensify until we are fused, at which point I know my time of prayer is complete. This can take anywhere from a minute to twenty minutes, it depends completely on how much I feel I need to sort out.

Here's an example of a prayer you might use to ask for assistance in finding a partner:

> *Dear God (or whatever term you feel most comfortable with), thank you for the connection I have to You, for the beauty in my life that has brought me awareness of your Holy Spirit. I ask that You clear my mind so that I may see what You want me to do, who You want me to meet, and how You want me to be. Take from me all that has held me back and shift my energy from fear to love so that I might find the partner who I'm looking forward to loving. Thank you for all that already is loving and miraculous in my life. Amen.*

Try praying for knowledge of God's will as opposed to specific outcomes, because in that all things are clear and imminently possible. If you are new to prayer or this is an uncomfortable process for you and you feel self-conscious, keep it simple. Like anything, start slowly and build. You can pray with even one word. Just dwell on the word God or Jesus or . . .

> Prayer is the force behind which all things already exist
> and are awaiting invitation.

After you pray, you want to stay open for flashes of inspiration and guidance. When you ask something of God, it is in every sense already on the way. Be flexible with what you are willing to see unfold, and remember that God always has a better plan for you than you could possibly have for yourself. The idea here is to just remain aware and alert for evidence of God's work. Impatience is your ego's way of declaring faithlessness; so do whatever it takes to get yourself out of the place of cynicism and doubt because as I mentioned earlier: your attitude and sense of surrendered expectation is what creates your reality. Being impatient implies that you don't trust that Grace is taking care of you and that you, rather than God, know best.

You know what happens when you hover by the phone, waiting for the call. It doesn't come. It's only when you go out and do something else and forget about it that the call finally comes. Know that when you've prayed, the energy has been put out, and you've done your part, and now the relationship is in God's hands. So walk away, do something else, and allow things to happen gracefully, without your constant impatience.

The Fusion Technique

Remember that we are three-dimensional beings; communion is something we can experience in body, mind, and spirit. Here's a technique I've developed to help you experience this full communion between your own energy and the energy of the Divine. I designed it because when I started out the process of manifesting a great relationship, I could sense that my psyche was not able to fathom the idea that something so great could happen to me, certainly not by my own resources. I knew that anything was possible if I could align my will with that of God's, but I also knew I had to feel it in my body as well as intellectually. I found that once I practiced this technique a few times, I really did feel the omnipotence of God working within me and in my life.

1. Close your eyes and get a sense of how your energy looks and feels, in terms of color, intensity, and vibrational frequency.

2. Imagine that you can see the energy of your prayer image. Try to feel it viscerally.

3. Imagine that your cells are opening up and becoming mutable. Picture yourself melting into the golden light of Grace.

4. Feel yourself expanding, vibrating with a higher level of energy.

5. Allow this feeling to spread throughout your body and into the deepest regions of your psyche. Experience in your bones, in your very being, that you are one with the Universal Mind.

When you realize that the power to transform any situation is within you, you can approach it with a gentle intention rather than from a needy stance. When you can experience the power of God within, you know with certainty and relief that good is on the way.

If you already have a prayer life and so far it looks like your prayers have not been answered, consider whether or not you are really ready to receive what you're asking for. If we can't handle receiving that for which we have asked, God will, in a sense, put it on the back burner for us until we are ready to expand and accommodate it. Later on in the process we will be fine-tuning our prayers to become more active programmers of what we want our partnership to be.

For now, let's move on to meditation. A lot of people confuse meditation with prayer. Let me explain how I see the difference. Meditation is a form of prayer but different in that it is more of a feminine and receptive practice, rather than that of actively praying. With prayer you focus on something specific, as if you are going in with a defined purpose. In meditation we seek to clear our minds, so that there's a blank canvas awaiting inspiration.

You might think of prayer as the asking and meditation as the listening. By praying you are asking for the relationship, while by meditating you are becoming the person who will draw that to you. Meditation is the most powerful tool I know for achieving a state of Grace.

Through meditation, your vibration rises and deepens at the same time, affecting your thoughts, perceptions, actions, and, ultimately, people's reaction to you. You initiate the Grace Consciousness within by dwelling on its presence, because anything you focus on, you give power to. We are able to access our own mystical, psychic powers through meditation, because the ego has moved aside and the superconscious, your Higher Power, is set free. It's as if you're creating a positive force field around you, which, by its very nature, draws in loving relationships and rejects lower energy situations.

It is said that we all have a superconscious, separate from the unconscious and conscious mind, a divine intelligence within. And when that element is activated, miracles can occur instantaneously. Again, evidence of the 'Mystical Third.'

∞

Consider Peggy: she had no man in her life and could not fore-see a change in her situation. She believed that, though she had children she loved, she would never have a complete life unless she found a partner. The children's father left them long ago, and Peggy would not have taken him back had he returned. She'd pretty much resigned herself to a life without romantic love by the time we met.

Peggy told me that she did not believe in any kind of miracle for herself. She was tired from life and didn't want to spend the energy to even hope things could be different. However, once in my workshop, she began to open up to possibilities other than what experience had shown her.

Peggy didn't have the time to go out and meet someone, and since she already knew everyone in her town, it didn't seem likely that Mr Right would pop out of a corner she didn't foresee. All logic pointed to Peggy staying the unfortunate, hardworking mom she was. Peggy began to use meditation to transport her from a spiritless life to one of a graceful existence. She prayed and meditated for twenty minutes a day for one month solid and felt a kind of release at the end of that time. She knew something was going to happen to her.

In one day, in one unexpected moment, she bumped into Jeff (who had popped out of an unforeseen corner!) and from that point on Peggy's life was different. The circumstances of their meeting could only have been arranged by Grace itself: In her busy life with her kids Peggy never had the time to chat with a stranger, but all at once she found the day's events leaving her alone for a bit, and she decided to go to the shops in town just to browse. Having a strange feeling of specialness without knowing why, Peggy enjoyed her afternoon. Sometime in the middle of it she happened to be looking at the same figurine on a shelf as a man, Jeff, and they struck up an enjoyable conversation about it, deciding to continue it at a coffee shop next door. It turned out that Jeff, from what he told Peggy, never went into shops like that and just happened that day to be there, looking for a gift for his sister he was in town visiting. They've been together ever since.

From that chance encounter, seemingly a minor co-incidence of fate but really a miracle in Peggy and Jeff's life, a deep, rewarding relationship developed. Because Peggy invited Grace in through prayer and meditation, her miracle came as if out of nowhere. Miracles are not always earth shattering, but can, in their quiet and chancelike way, change our lives profoundly.

How to Meditate

I would suggest that you start meditating for about three minutes at first – use a kitchen timer or watch with an alarm so you don't have to be preoccupied with when to end the meditation. After you feel comfortable with three minutes, work up to five minutes and, eventually, twenty minutes twice a day.

Try to find a quiet place for your meditation, a place where you feel comfortable that can become a sanctuary for your spiritual practice. It doesn't have to be a separate room or grand space. At one point in my life, I was so desperate for quiet and privacy that my meditation space was my closet! Consider being out in nature, or in a church or temple or, better yet, a quiet corner of your home. But wherever it is, make it special somehow by adding a few elements of your spiritual life to remind you of why you're there: a picture of God as you understand Him, a candle, crystals, or a tiny bunch of flowers. When you create the space, action will follow.

Start by lying down, as I described in Step 1 (see page 24).

If you feel, though, that you want to take it to a more advanced level, you can try sitting cross-legged on the floor with a pillow underneath you to tilt you slightly forward. Keep your spine erect and straight, as it serves to channel energy directly through you. Breathe in deeply through your nose while expanding your belly and upon exhaling, make a slight sound of the breath being balanced between your nose and your throat while your belly contracts. Choose a word or phrase, perhaps even a mantra, to focus your attention on, such as 'I am' or 'peace' or 'om' (according to Eastern wisdom, *om* is the sound with which all of life resonates).

As your thoughts come up, let them waft by without pinning your attention to them. Know that, when you come out of your meditation, you can deal with everything, but for now just let all of your concerns go. Picture yourself surrounded by golden light and infused with a peace that empties out any anxiety or tension. Focus solely on the breath and your repeated mantra, disregarding the pull of your ego's chatter. Do this with the intent to empty your mind completely, so that you become an open field of placid energy. When in this place of total serenity you become a clear conduit for Grace to enter into your being.

Another good way to bypass your regular thinking and open up to potential is to lose yourself in a meditative *action*. By this I mean to completely commit yourself to an action, whether it be ironing clothes or riding a bike. If you can completely focus on what you're doing, on the particular actions required, and shut out all your mind chatter, you will enter into a zone of clarity and openness.

There is nothing that is not possible when your energy is aligned and infused with that of Grace. Keep the channel open and love will appear!

Seven Everyday Tips to Assist in Step 2, Inviting Grace in:

1. Copy your favorite prayer into your daily agenda or onto your computer screen, wherever you'll see it often.

2. When you're feeling spiritually empty, take a nature walk to remind yourself that Grace is all around us.

3. Go to a church or a temple to get yourself in a spiritual mode.

4. With every person you meet today, say a quick prayer under your breath to see the Grace within them.

5. Carry a spiritual trinket with you as a constant reminder of your intention.

6. Create a ritual by opening up a window in your home and symbolically usher in the energy of spirit.

7. When a problem arises, write it down and put it into a box labeled 'God's Business.' Give it time and then come back to it when you feel the energy has shifted by your surrender.

Know What You Want and Why

> *When making a decision of minor importance, I have always found it advantageous to consider all the pros and cons. In vital matters, however, such as the choice of a mate or a profession, the decision should come from the unconscious, from somewhere within ourselves. In the important decisions of personal life, we should be governed, I think, by the deep inner needs of our nature.*
>
> —SIGMUND FREUD

So far, I've been helping you prepare, on an internal level, for a miracle. We've been talking about calming the body, stilling the mind, and opening yourself to spirit. Because what we think and what we speak of is actually the seed for what happens in our lives, now it's time to begin to think about what you want in a partner and why. The seed, your desire for partnership, germinates from the continual energy you put into it. In order to draw the right partner to you, it is absolutely essential that you be conscious of what it is you want. The more clear you are on what you want, the better the universe is able to mirror your desires.

THE UNIVERSE IS A MIRROR

We are all sending messages about ourselves all the time; people know who we are instantly and respond in kind. We intuitively sense what is real in each other; indeed the universe also picks up fraudulent affirmations. To begin the inner shift you must get very clear on where you already stand, and take a hard look at what's important to you.

We often seek out people who will fill a need in us rather than complement our higher selves. At this point in the process it's worth asking yourself whether what you desire in a relationship has more to do with rounding out your incomplete self or mirroring your best self. For starters, people can sense neediness and it actually repels the very quality you wish to find. Further, being completed by someone else, however good it might feel at the time, always leaves you needing more and more to maintain the illusion of being whole. When we are whole, we attract the same quality in another person. And so divine partnership is about finding someone who testifies to our own personal perfection rather than fostering our dependence.

I want to stress again the importance of working *within your own self* on those qualities you seek in others. For instance, if you are looking for someone 'successful' because you don't feel up to par in that department, you would do well to take the time to sharpen your own sense of success. Success can be defined and experienced in many ways. You don't have to go after the very same brand of success that you want in a partner, but you nevertheless have to own the quality and sensation of success. I mean, would a really successful person want to be burdened with your desperate need to latch on to them? No. So just know that no one is going to *complete* you; they can't do that job for you! They can only bring out and add to who you already are.

Take a look at the following Qualities Inventory – and please add your own items if you don't find them here – in order to help you (and the universal mind) get some clarity about what it is you are looking for in a partner. Choose ten of these and put them in the order of their priority to you:

Qualities Inventory

- Kind
- Respectable
- Good looking
- Intelligent
- Gentle
- Daring
- Extroverted
- Introverted
- Edgy
- Traveler
- Quiet
- Studious

- Creative
- Animal lover
- Vulnerable
- Confident
- Bad boy image
- Older than you
- Same age
- Successful
- Virile
- Perfectionist
- Mellow
- Social

- Emotionally available
- Artsy
- Funny
- Honest
- Tall
- Thin
- Muscular
- Athletic

- Ambitious
- Independent
- Wealthy
- Short
- Tasteful
- Wants children
- Has children
- Divorced

Take a Closer Look

Now, one by one, examine each quality for the underlying characteristic that your soul is seeking. For example, if you chose as your top priority 'kindness,' ask yourself what it is about being kind that you desire and are attracted to. On first glance it might appear to be obvious, as kindness feels good and comfortable. But close your eyes and allow the feeling of someone's kindness to fill you up. What is it that you experience? Perhaps it is a feeling of safety, of being accepted or validated. Or maybe the kindness of your partner allows you to feel confident to shine in your own individual way. You can also tap into your memory to find where there is a wound or an inspiration around this quality. The more you deepen your understanding of what you want, the more clearly your energy can connect with it.

Because, as you have seen by now, you will always attract the feeling, the *vibration*, of exactly what you ask for, you will fare better if you truly connect with the underlying qualities of what it is you seek. If you have a vague, ambiguous desire, and don't put much thought into it, then the relationship that shows up will have that same undefined quality that will not ultimately satisfy you. It's as if you would pick up the phone to call a delivery service but not tell them which restaurant or what kind of food you want. All you know is that you're hungry, perhaps even starving; but when the food arrives it's not at all what you had a hankering for.

> In order to be fulfilled and to satisfy your core needs and desires, you must be clear and articulate what you want. Life does not present that which doesn't resonate with you.

When we radiate the energy of who we are and what we want, the universe simply gives us the experience that confirms our belief. To change that which is reflected back to us we must tweak the energy we put out. When we put out strong loving feelings about our desires and ourselves, we will be recognized and answered by the powers that be with benevolence and love.

Relationships are an excellent way that we can witness our soul's growth at work. You can't simply snap your fingers and affirm you're someone that you're not. To fake the energy is to send mixed messages; you must first shift on the most fundamental level. By using the checklist on page 82, we begin to shape the energy which we wish to see manifest in a partner.

∞

Meet Jessie: at thirty-six, a single mother, she wanted badly to have a man in her life, not only to be a partner but to be a father to her eight-year-old son. Whenever she thought of a man, this was her primary focus, leaving aside many of the other qualities she usually found attractive. Feeling that her son was the most important component of her life, Jessie was almost unaware of her own passions.

Dating had always been difficult because of her responsibilities as a mother, and Jessie never seemed to find a man who 'fit' into the 'role' she was looking for.

She went out with a man who seemed to really enjoy spending time with her son, and was perfect as a mentor for him. But something just wasn't there for her, and Jessie spent long hours thinking about it while driving to and from work, trying to justify staying in the relationship with him. Eventually the man stopped calling, sensing her disinterest, despite the fact that everything she was saying was that she was happy. Jessie was happy for her son, but not for herself.

Unaware that she would have to reconcile her son's needs with her own, Jessie went from one man to another, but always things would dissolve in a vague dissatisfaction. She began to despair that she'd never find the right man and spend her life alone as a single mother, her own needs forever left unmet.

This feeling was the precursor to her solving the problem, because she started to really think deeply about her own needs.

As we got further into our work together, Jessie began to list out for herself the qualities she wanted in a man and in their relationship. She really craved artistic expression in someone, a strong sense of inner worth that made it possible for him to laugh at and enjoy himself, and the ability to give and receive love without any game-playing attached. Passion was important to her as well, and even if he could be a good father figure to her son, he would also need to be a lover to her.

There were many other qualities she began to add, minor and major, that at first seemed like a 'wish list.' Interestingly, as she thought about the qualities she wanted, she realized there were ones she didn't care about, even though they were virtuous. She wasn't looking for a 'superman,' just someone with whom she and her son could truly be comfortable. But still, Jessie doubted that she would ever be able to find someone that fulfilled all these criteria. She didn't realize that that doubt was merely coming from her past experience and disappointment, and not from her ability to magnetize a future reality that fit her needs like a glove.

Then the magic started happening in Jessie's life: her 'ideal man' began to take shape in her mind and took on a life of his own. As this happened she became more and more comfortable with him, the idea of him, and let herself relax from her doubts. Her specific needs, which at first made him seem like a mail-order husband, began to seem natural to her, and she slowly became willing to entertain the thought that she wasn't crazy to want all that in her man.

Jessie began to see herself in a relationship with this 'man' and visualized all kinds of interactions with him and, conversely, she *stopped wanting or demanding him from the universe. It was a matter of becoming open to the clearly defined idea of him, and when she actually met and became involved with a man who met her various needs, she was surprised and enthralled because he was different than her 'idea' of him and yet the same.*

An important component of Jessie's 'enlightenment' was her willingness. She was never before open to the possibility that she could in fact be so lucky to find a man with all the qualities she deemed important. But then she became willing to be open to the possibility that she *could* get what she actually wanted and things started to become clear. I hate to contradict my grandma, but whereas she always warned that the road to Hell is paved with good intentions, I would say the way out is by a willingness to change, to be receptive in a whole new way, and to be in the world without being chained to your old and familiar limitations.

There are always reasons to stop us from moving forward in our development as human beings, and certainly as partners. Part of the process of self-actualizing is meeting our fears and demons head on, grappling with them and coming out stronger and more powerful. There is nothing in life worthwhile that has been gained easily and without great emotional effort. Perhaps we are given these obstacles to overcome, in order that we might know our strength for having successfully overcome them.

BE WILLING TO HAVE EXACTLY WHAT YOU WANT

Let's try an exercise. I call it the Willing to Be Willing exercise. I want you to list three things that would need to change in order for you to find your partner. Under each thing, list the reasons why you don't do it.

Things that would need to change.

For example:

1. I need to be more outgoing.

    a. I'm shy by nature.

    b. I'm afraid of rejection.

    c. I never liked bars.

1. _____

    a.

    b.

    c.

2. _____

    a.

    b.

    c.

3. _____

a.

b.

c.

Using my example, you would ask yourself, is not being outgoing a valid reason for remaining unfulfilled? If you are falling back on excuses because you are afraid to risk pushing yourself, you might want to ask yourself what's more important: being right (about the excuse) or moving forward (by risking change)? I'm not saying that you have to figure everything out at once, just that, in order to have the change occur, you need to be Willing to Be Willing.

Mantra
I am willing to see things differently.

Now let's do a mental exercise where we set up a willingness to let go of old behavioral patterns, therefore freeing ourselves to have new frames of reference about our ability to be involved with someone in a loving relationship. Remember, this is not about forcefully changing what has been natural for us all along, but about being open to the idea that we are more than the personalities that have resulted from our historical experiences.

Hold in your mind the first of your three reasons that keep you back from each of the things you'd like to change. Going with our example about not being outgoing enough, in your mind's eye, go to what you decided would have to change in order to unblock the energy. First see yourself being shy, and now picture yourself with a few people around you that you feel comfortable with. In your mind's eye, see yourself chatting and laughing with and receiving admiration from these people. Expand that vision so that it encompasses more people, and as each person is added to your vision, notice how you are still comfortable and actually enjoying the company of such a diverse crowd. At this point, realize that making a shift in your energy is not as impossible as you had thought. Sometimes all it takes is being able to see yourself differently than you've grown accustomed to. One also has to be at least willing to have the shift occur. Your willingness opens the door, and fulfillment naturally follows.

Perhaps in doing this exercise you discover that you really are not willing to change something about yourself, such as admitting your shortcomings and dealing with them. Change is often scary and uncomfortable, and we all move at our own pace and in our own perfect way. When we expect this about ourselves, and trust that situations and circumstances will arise to continue giving us the opportunity to shift our energy, we can have compassion for ourselves. Knowing that change is always waiting for us to access its miracle, we can be patient and therefore act out of love rather than fear. Simply be willing to be willing to move through what is uncomfortable. When your mind is open, there is a magnetic energy that draws to you like-minded individuals.

Now complete the rest of this exercise with your emotional energy behind it. Fill in the blanks for each reason why you thought you couldn't change, with your own ideas about how you are willing to.

Example:

1. I am not an outgoing person, so I am willing to accept the possibility that, in my own way, I will meet the world halfway.

    a. I am shy, but I am willing to see that as a charming asset.

    b. I am afraid of rejection, but I'm willing to expose myself anyway, trusting that I will survive no matter what.

    c. I don't like bars, but I am willing to explore another social situation that is comfortable to me, such as taking a class.

Now write these responses to your own.

1. _____

    a.

    b.

    c.

2. _____

    a.

    b.

    c.

3. _____

    a.

    b.

    c.

Remember, just being Willing to Be Willing is enough to affect change.

LISTEN TO YOUR INNER GUIDANCE

It's important to have a clear idea of who you want to be with in your mind before you put your energy into asking for it. Only you will know what type of person connects with you – no one else can dictate that to you. We have all had the experience of meeting someone we thought would make us happy, and finding out they weren't really right for us at all. We can avoid this hit-or-miss approach by following a few easy steps.

Your best ally in gaining clarity about this is your own inner knowingness. No matter how covered over it might be by harmful or painful experiences, or clashing with what the outside world expects, you still have instinctive impulses that will never steer you wrong when you listen to them. You must only rediscover, and hone, what is already there.

Learning to listen to this inner compass is essential to attracting what will nourish you on all levels. What is that *knowingness*? People experience it in different ways, but you could say first and foremost that it is a feeling attribute. Your feelings about someone, any insights you have, intuition, or deep certainties, are ways the soul guides you. They come before rationalization. Knowingness is simply a gut feeling.

> Inner knowing does not result from a balance sheet of pros and cons. It's a kind of silent, pre-lingual inclination.

Your inner guidance is, in a way, a call from God, and is always accompanied by a deep sense that what you are doing is right. Say you have a business idea that would not only serve you well but also all those who come in contact with it; there will be a click of recognition that you are indeed on the right path. Inner guidance has nothing to do with linear thinking – it has to do with the soul's connection to that which is good and pure and right for you.

This may sound like a lot of shoulds. 'Should' is a word I don't like to use much because it implies that our own internal judgment is invalid and must be discounted. Using 'should' gradually undermines us, so that we no longer trust ourselves. So when you say to yourself, 'I should like Harry because he has a good job and he loves kids and he would never leave me . . .' note that you're not coming from your instinctive desire to appreciate Harry, but from a place of deferment to external worldly reason. God does not work through such a pedestrian set of assumptions about what's 'appropriate'; the process is far deeper than that.

In a minute we'll get to how to decipher whether or not your feelings are true 'knowing' feelings or have other hidden roots. But first, a simple example of cutting quickly through to inner guidance:

∽

Emily and John had been living together for a year or so, and were generally happy. But there was one problem that kept gnawing at their serenity – they couldn't agree on where to live. They had moved from one town to the next, finding dissatisfaction each time but getting tired of the constant upheaval. They'd been in a beautiful town for a few months but were frustrated with the employment situation and the crime rate, which was dangerously high at that time. Even though they had a comfortable apartment, it was a struggle to make ends meet and it didn't seem like it would get any better in the near future. They felt good there, but the odds seemed stacked against them.

So, following their urge to make a decision, which may have given them as much trouble as help over the months, they took a trip to another beautiful, though larger town to see if they might want to move there. The conundrum was, the two towns were very similar in a lot of ways; each had pros and cons that balanced each other out. The rent was lower in the new town, but moving there would cost more money; employment was possibly better in the larger town, but they couldn't be sure from a quick visit, and to top it off it was springtime and both places were absolutely enchanting, seducing the couple equally with sheer aesthetic beauty. They walked around weighing it out, getting their minds into a fever of doubt and anxiety. To take one would be to lose all of the other. And what if they made the wrong choice? They couldn't pick up and leave again any time soon. The decision had to be the right one. Finally, after a tortuous day wandering around town, they ended up in a park and it was getting late. Time had run out. Their minds were full of arguments 'for' and 'against.'

In a moment of inspiration John recalled an exercise I taught him about gauging our instincts. Since the perfect home was more important for Emily, he asked her to stand in a quiet place in the center of the new town and close her eyes. When she did this John told her to let all her thoughts about the decision go. He said that on her left lay the new town and her right the old. Then he asked her to let her body 'decide' by stepping in either direction, and that would be the right place. Emily was not to think about it at all. So he said 'decide' and she, without hesitation, stepped to the left. It was the new town. Then they laughed and realized with great relief that within them was the instinct for the right decision, which their subsequent experience bore out.

John and Emily's story shows that when we want to get to the root of how we really feel about something the answer is in our Trinity Self, not only in our mind, but in our body and soul as well.

DISCERN INNER TRUTH FROM OLD FEARS

You may sometimes wonder if your gut feelings are really based on the truth or if they manifest from a dysfunctional place of fear. Everyone has experienced wishful thinking, worried feelings, and impulsive thoughts. These are natural states of mind and one need not feel guilty for having them. Sometimes what may seem to be an exciting connection with someone is in fact a reconnection of old, neurotic behavior. Look at the person in front of you and notice what's going on inside your body and in your heart. Does this person bring a sense of peace and well-being with him/her, or do all of your old fears seem to come to the surface?

Instinct or inner guidance is the place inside us that is part of the great universal flow of energy. It is the natural way we are, beneath any artifice, and it always serves us well. The way to access your instinct is to get very quiet, listen to your body, and pay attention to wisdom that seems to come from your Higher Mind. It will resonate with a 'rightness' that will be clear and strong. When the right partner comes along, you will feel it in the highest part of your being.

> You will be guided by the universal source, of which you contain a part, to your right partner. This instinctual attention is born of the Grace within.

EXERCISE: TAPPING THE WISDOM OF THE BODY

Here's an exercise that can help you clarify what your true self desires and give you a sample of how inner guidance can operate. It's based on the principle of applied kinesiology, the idea that we can often best get to the innate knowledge that the body holds by bypassing the conscious mind. When we ask ourselves a question, a weak or strong response to pressure on the closed fist, remarkably, gives us an excellent window into the body's wisdom.

1. Hold your left hand in a fist, elbow tucked in, parallel to the ground.

2. Set up a point of reference: affirm something you know to be true (such as 'My name is . . .').

3. With your right, open palm try to push your fist down. You won't be able to push the fist very far down because

the strength in your fist confirms the truth of your statement.

4. Now take the question at hand, such as 'John is a good person for me.'

5. If your left fist drops down considerably more than it did with your earlier 'truth' statement, you'll know what you're saying is that, indeed, John is not good for you. The answer is always silently waiting within us.

Once you realize you're heading down a path grounded in truth, and you relax into a sense of trust that your desires will be coming from love and faith, you may be surprised at the ease with which someone new fits into your life.

BUT WHY DO WE WANT WHAT WE WANT?

After you get some clarity about what you want in a partner, it's also important to understand why. For instance, if you desire someone who is loyal and kind, what is it you are really after? What's the underlying quality? Is it that you seek security or the upper hand? Or perhaps a sanctuary in your life? Or maybe that you just don't want to be challenged. We all want things for reasons that may seem on the surface self-evident, but in fact we are driven by deeper and more spiritual needs. You see, when you know the truth of what drives you, you are able to cut through the rationalizations that can be misleading, and respond to what is truly important to you. So let's go deeper than just loyalty and kindness and consider that, perhaps, what resonates with you is a soulful monogamous relationship in which you can flourish into your full potential as a spiritual human being.

It is always helpful to state your desired qualities in the positive, rather than saying what you don't want. The clear intention draws to you the *like* (or similar) energy instead of the more confused vibration of merely avoiding what you don't want. For example, saying 'I don't want a cheater' calls in the energy of 'cheater.' What you resist persists, so be careful what you defend against.

> The importance of knowing what your goals mean to you is so that you can build a strong foundation of self-identification, to which a natural partner is drawn.

Since we are all spiritually and physically connected, it makes sense that the more in touch we are with our own deeper nature, the more easily we can connect on a deep level with a partner. The more we understand what really drives us, the better able we are to visualize our right partner.

Consider what happens when you meet someone in the process of dating: how you *feel* when thinking about that person will tell you whether they are healthy for you or not. If you feel a sense of delight (delight is a marker for the soul's truth; it's never wrong), you know you're on the right track. If you feel crazy and loopy and drunk with love, you are probably projecting onto the other person. If this is the case, you will inevitably be tested by your Higher Power to see if you are *really* moving forward with your growth. If you are doing this work, you will now have the opportunity to say 'no thank you' to an old pattern. Even though the old attraction might be there, you will now be able to recognize it as part of what you need to leave behind. Of course, sometimes you just need to go around that track one more time. I'm just asking you to be clear about what it is you want and why.

So what do you do if you feel resistance when you contemplate being with this new person in your life? Now you need to be able to determine if the resistance is legitimate, meaning that the person really isn't right for you, that they don't respond to the truth of who you are, or if the resistance is coming from a fear of actually being with someone good for you, which is a form of self-sabotage.

You'll know it is self-sabotage if when asking yourself why you feel that the relationship will fail, you come upon the feeling that you aren't worthy of it. If you think there's no way you can manifest what you want, that there's just a wall between you and fulfillment, then know this:

There are no walls that miracles cannot move if you simply have the willingness to transform.

Question why you feel the way you do; you will get an answer. You may not like it, but you would be wise to listen. We may have to ask why again, or again and again, to get to the root of it. When you do finally know the truth of it, the walls will disappear.

If you are feeling a legitimate resistance, a sense that you are being steered away by a higher force, remain open to another direction. Validate your fears by listening to them and then let them go, knowing that they no longer serve you. In the meantime, take care to do things that honor yourself, things that reaffirm your willingness to move forward.

Remember, knowing why you want to be with a certain kind of person is about getting very clear on what essentially serves your higher self. And in doing that, you are also serving your potential partner's higher self, too. Not only are you worth it, but he/she deserves to get the best from you, too. For example, if you are with someone and you don't know particularly why you like them, you are not honoring their uniqueness. And, certainly, if you can't identify how someone serves such a high purpose in your life, then you are not ideally suited after all.

KNOW YOUR INTENTIONS

Let's talk about intentions for a moment. Our intentions are our purposes, what we mean and are motivated by. We are conduits of energy and our intentions create, form, and mold that energy. In other words, we bring into being who we are by who we *intend* to be. Like electricity to a radio, our *intention* is the 'on' switch that allows the energy to flow through. If we are not conscious of our intentions, our energy becomes unfocused and weak. Less magnetic.

A big part of knowing your intention is getting to the heart of what is motivating your desire. This will tell you whether or not it has harmony with your surrounding world.

> **What you intend is what you'll create, even if you're not aware of doing it, or aware of wanting it.**

Intention is like an invisible force, like a wind filling a sail that moves us through life, manifesting by *setting up* patterns, coincidences, behaviors, and relationships.

Intentions, though, like the motivations for goals, can be conflicting.

Here's an example:

∞

Fiona was involved in a very destructive relationship with a man she could not trust and who treated her very badly. She came to me out of desperation, seemingly unable to break away. No matter how many times she tried to leave him, she kept return-ing. She knew the man was bad for her, holding her down and making her feel unworthy. She drank more than was healthy, lost weight, and basically let her life fall apart. A lot of her own friends pretty much abandoned her, as they felt helpless and hurt watching her going through it. Fiona knew she had to get out and felt all the more ashamed because she couldn't.

What she didn't understand at the time was that by dealing with this man's abuse, and trying to help him fix his own problems, she was avoiding her own. She thought her problems stemmed from him, but of course they were much older and more firmly entrenched than this present relationship. She was merely allowing him to distract her from dealing with her own issues. By being complicit in his drama she absented herself from taking responsibility for her own life. Even though Fiona thought she intended on making things good with her man, her true intention was to avoid dealing with her own issues and problems.

Once I helped her to see what her real intention was – to avoid working on herself – she was no longer able to point the finger at 'the perpetrator' and blame him. He had only (unknowingly of course) provided her with the distraction she sought. Embarrassed by the now-evident lack of responsibility she had taken for her life, Fiona began focusing on herself and dealing with her demons. She no longer needed the 'bad boyfriend' to fill her time and attention. Over time, she became a self-actualized woman and therefore attracted the same healthy sort of man!

Coming to consciously understand your intentions leads you to make a clear choice, and once that choice is made you won't be able to justify fooling yourself any longer.

If you want something to change, it's important to know why you want it and how it will affect everyone involved.

INTEGRATE YOUR DESIRES

If you are to make any progress in magnetizing a partner, you'll need to be able to clearly define and follow integrated goals. What are integrated goals? They are goals which serve each aspect of the Trinity Self; they serve your outer needs as well as your inner ones. You accept them for their superficial value (such as good sex is fun!) and honor them for their profundity (such as sexual union brings forth a deep spiritual union).

First, you need to make sure your goals aren't merely compromises that try to satisfy too many conflicting sides to have any real force of their own. If they are, your spirit won't have enough energy or enthusiasm to push them through and make them manifest. The soul knows when it's being lied to and responds with indifference. Because it is the momentum of energetic force building upon itself that carries you to be in the exact right place at the right time. But this momentum is hindered if your goals are the result of a committee meeting; you will have bureaucratic energy – apathetic and scattered.

Something you feel you 'should' do isn't necessarily a genuine motivation: a 'should' is only right for you if it comes from your own inner barometer and desire. For example, thinking you should be with a partner who gives you three children and a nice house might be a projection of what society is telling you to be. Just because commercials tell you that you 'should' have a perfectly slim body (and drinking a particular product will get you there) doesn't make it an integrated, healthy goal to be fulfilled. If that's the reason why you want to be slim, to fit into someone else's ideal, you'll always be in a battle because your soul will know it's a shallow desire and doesn't come from a grounded, healthy place.

An integrated goal about having perfect weight will come from a deep desire to be healthy, and/or to live out a higher part of your self through that body. Your soul will know the difference and give you the energy for the manifestation, where before it would have fought against it. The same goes for relationships: if the internal desire to connect with someone is integrated with the 'picture' of what it could look and feel like, it will manifest. But if it's the picture without the essence of soulful expression, you'll have a tough time feeling fulfilled.

Again, the quality of delight will shine through when the desire integrates the essence and the exterior. Something that is real, coming from within, will give you hints of delightful anticipation. You'll have positive feelings when you think about attaining a legitimate goal, as compared to fearful resistance if it's false. Your body is naturally delightful, alive, and in tune with the universe. When your decisions give you this feeling, you know you've made the right ones.

Delight, rather than infatuation, is an important marker that things are directed from your Higher Power.

ACT WITH INTEGRITY

It is also very important that your goals have *integrity*. By this I mean that they are for the good of everyone involved. Everything (your desires, intentions, actions, etc.) has to be morally, ethically, and spiritually aligned. That's not to say that everyone has to be perfect right away, but that, at the end of the day, everyone's highest good is served.

An example of an action that doesn't have integrity would be trying to force someone to fall in love with you. An integrated desire doesn't manipulate other people in any way; instead, it naturally brings out the best in everyone.

We attract the essence, not the details. So when you act from integrity, you may find a special someone falling in love with you naturally; there is no need to trick or manipulate. The consequences are in tune with the *integrity* of the universe.

Once you've defined and clarified your goals, and you understand the deeper meaning of them, you'll want to examine the road ahead. What challenges might you encounter along the way? How can you best deal with them? You'll want to cultivate a certainty about your direction (and the exercises will show you how to do this) that will permeate your actions so that any unexpected difficulties don't derail you.

And here is the good news: you may not need to work at it as hard as you think. With a desire that is true and intentions that are clear, you are in tune with the universal force and the resistance will disappear. It will be natural for you to succeed in attracting a perfect partner. This is where miracles and Grace come into play. Higher Power will unfold into your life in the guise of luck, good timing, and coincidence that will make the partnership seem magical.

It's important to assimilate the expectation of miracles into your belief structure so that their unfolding will be natural and graceful.

CREATE A TIME FRAME THAT WORKS FOR YOU

It's also important to have a sense of timing about your desires. What are the things you really would like to have right away, and what are the things you feel are waiting for you on the horizon? For example, you might not want to meet THE ONE right away. Perhaps you want to date and experience this new power that you have for a couple of years. Or maybe you have some career projects you'd like to complete before you move into family life. Also, at the same time as creating a time frame, try to think of these things in terms of their attainability. Can they be had quickly, or do they need to develop slowly and gently? How comfortable are you with things manifesting, and how easily can you handle everything that goes along with it? You might need to warm up to living in close quarters with someone or sharing vacations and such. There's a paradox here in that you need to prioritize your goals and be realistic about them (this will help you define them, indirectly) while at the same time making room for the uncensored miracles that are on the way. As they say, 'Luck is when opportunity intersects with preparation.' Do the footwork, of course, but let the grand plan present itself in its own perfect way.

EXERCISE: ARTICULATING WHAT YOU WANT

Here is an exercise to help you articulate and understand your desires and goals. Complete the following fill-in-the-blank statements. Be very honest with yourself, and if it takes several times to get to the heart of the matter, don't worry. When you write out an answer and it doesn't feel complete, or click as being wholly true, ask yourself why and write out *that* answer. You can continue with this line of thinking until the truth becomes clear to you. Save your answers for future reference.

Fill in the blanks:

- What I want in a partner is _____

- The underlying characteristics are_____

- Knowing the underlying characteristics, my goal is now

_____

- My conscious intentions in the area of relationship are

_____

- My unconscious intentions are_____

- My transformation would affect the people around me in that _____

- This transformation is positive for my spiritual growth because_____

- My desired transformation has integrity because_____

- I __ **am/am not** __ willing to have this miracle manifest.

Now you know what you truly desire, and why. This critical understanding will enable you to move into the next phase of the process of attracting a spiritual partnership, clearing the way.

Just remember, the universe reflects back to you who you really think you are and what it is you 'call' for at this point in time. So be specific and clear. Be Willing to Be Willing to have a change occur, listen to the internal messages that are always present, and allow yourself to be guided to a deep understanding of yourself and the desires that drive you.

Let's do a meditation now to bring this inner knowing into focus. The Trinity Self needs to digest and encode this information, and there is no better way to listen for guidance than by meditating.

You may want to read through this first and then meditate, or record it in your own voice to assist in guiding you through.

INTERNAL BLUEPRINT MEDITATION

Relax and get very comfortable.

Breathe in and center yourself. Breathe out all the distractions that keep you from focusing. Let them go now. We are here not only to create an opening, but also an energetic environment where your desires manifest.

Now let's focus on what you want to manifest. This particular phase of Expecting a Miracle is about drawing to you a perfect partner through clarity of intention. In your mind, define for yourself what a wonderful relationship would look like. Perhaps at first thought you envision the two of you being in a beautiful home, cooking together. Or maybe you would be traveling to exotic places around the world. Create your image of a thriving partnership in whatever way seems ideal to you. Your feelings will grow the reality, so you really want to make it live inside of you.

Now imagine being together with someone who fits the general description, and then let's take it to a deeper level. What are the essential qualities behind the image of your desired relationship? Is it the opportunity to connect with someone in a deeply committed way? Maybe it's a feeling of safety or security you're after, or to have a lifelong friend with whom you share everything. You see, being with this particular partner, or idea of them, isn't just about having someone in your life, it's more about expanding your heart and opening more to love.

Imagine yourself, now, being in a room with your mate. Think of the checklist again, and go through all the qualities they would have. Keep thinking and make mental notes, letting the idea of the partner you want develop gradually, naturally, until it is very specific. The more you give your subconscious to work with, the more powerfully the energy will be magnetizing them towards you.

Hold the image of your perfect mate in your mind. Get comfortable and familiar with it, and begin to see yourself in a relationship. Take the next three minutes to create the blueprint of what you want the relationship to look like. Then slowly open your eyes and put this book down for three days to allow the new energy to settle in.

The next step is about purifying yourself in order to make room for the miracle to happen. Once you are clear about what you want in a relationship and why, you have to clear the way for it to unfold.

Seven Everyday Tips to Assist in Step 3, Knowing What You Want and Why:

1. Remove the word 'should' from your vocabulary.

2. Before purchasing anything, ask yourself why you *really* want it. This gets you in the habit of understanding your motives.

3. Read books and watch movies to see how qualities you'd like to have show up in fictional characters.

4. Keep a journal of your feelings about events in your life and analyze them.

5. Spend some money on something you would have thought frivolous but makes you feel special.

6. When someone gives you a compliment, sincerely take it and believe that they mean it.

7. Give yourself a task that's a little difficult but not completely daunting, and upon its completion you'll realize how capable you really are.

STEP 4

Clear the Way

I know of no other advice than this: Go within and scale the depths of your being from which your very life springs forth.

—RAINER MARIA RILKE

In Step 3, we did some very important work toward helping you find your miracle partnership – figuring out what you want in a relationship and why. Now it's time to turn our attention to why you don't already have one. If being in love is so important, why in the world haven't you managed to work it out?

Let me say right here that I don't believe in bad luck, and I don't think it's all a matter of destiny. I think we all have our potential, that which God intends for us, and that we work with Him to actualize what's possible. What stands in your way now are the blocks that you accumulated through your life experiences. It actually doesn't matter what caused the blocks – traumatic experiences from childhood, learned behavior that doesn't work, fear of the unknown – the solution is the same. You first have to understand what stops you, what holds you back, and then change it. Sound too simple? I promise you it's neither too simple nor too hard. It is simply a kind of personal work that takes courage and the willingness to look very deeply at your strategies and behaviors. Once you identify the behaviors, and decide to change them, the change process itself flows quite naturally. Please read on.

What We Do

Most of us carry and act out on a lot of negativity without even realizing it. We *really don't know* we're doing it. And it all flows from the fact that we don't really believe we deserve a good relationship. In fact for many of us the pattern of negative relating is so deeply ingrained, we sabotage ourselves without knowing it. Remember, I'm not talking about a logical, intellectual process; I'm talking about how our unconscious navigates, *unbeknownst* to us, into self-fulfilling prophecies. What we don't think we deserve, *we will not allow to happen*.

In a way, what we do by letting relationships fall apart, or carefully skirting intimacy, is to escape pushing ourselves to deal with the fundamental conflicts that run us. Instead of admitting our shortcomings, we work very hard to save face. By nature we are 'displacers,' afraid to take responsibility for our part in creating our own unhappiness. We are afraid that we will be punished for any wrongdoing, or even wrong thinking, if not by the old image of a vengeful god, then by the ensuing drama we create by our mistakes.

One of the best ways to avoid culpability is to project guilt onto whomever we have dated or been with in the past. If we can point a finger and say that it's the other guy's fault, we don't have to look at ourselves in the mirror. Of course if we never look at ourselves, we can't change the situation, because we certainly can't control what other people do. Really, we only have ourselves to work with. So let's dissect what the ego has constructed in order to keep us as far away from truth as possible. Remember, the ego is our small self, the one created out of fear, which tries desperately to stay in control and keep us unaware of the benevolent force of love.

Mantra

I am willing to look within and accept everything I discover.

When we look back at old relationships, we can usually see a pattern or a common dynamic at play. This, of course, is not a coincidence, but the work of our subconscious reenacting old pains that probably issued from a childhood wound. No childhood is perfect: we either didn't get enough attention or we got smothered by attention or we didn't find our own direction because of the strong person-alities who cared for us. Whatever it was, a crack in our sense of well-being was made, forming a scar. Unless tended to, these old buried hurts will continue to control us. We will be drawn to people and situations who will assist us in finally bringing the conflict to a head. We choose someone who will dance the dance with us. We can feel them from across the room without knowing a thing about them: it's as if a karmic force is pulling at us. We lock eyes, our shadow selves recognize the potential in each other, and we're off.

You see, what the ego sees as *finding* itself – in a partner – really amounts to being enmeshed in a codependent relationship. We find a partner and at first it feels like magic, like we're breathing for the first time. Our heart swells with the feeling of finally being seen and understood. We feel like we're finally being nurtured, satiated at last. We think that person (poor unwitting soul!) will fulfill our every need, and we love who we are through their per-ception of us. Of course then, we have to *become* exactly who it is they want us to be, in order to keep their love. Oh, how exhausting . . .

We become completely dependent on the Other validat-ing, agreeing with, and giving us purpose. We know at last who we are and where we stand in the world. Their priorities are our priorities, and we expect that they'll know how to fill our every need. Impossible! But just like a toddler not getting what he wants, we feel devastated and throw a tantrum at the slightest sign of independence.

This is obviously not healthy, and soon enough the illusion of perfection wears off and at the end of the day we feel more alone than ever. It's like eating white sugar: at first you feel the rush of being satiated, but you quickly take a dive into feeling more hungry and empty than ever.

It's amazing how what seemed absolutely perfect can morph into something with so many shortcomings practically overnight. And at this point the other person doesn't have a chance because no matter what they do, all of our preconceived notions that were secretly awaiting confirmation (the big 'Aha! I knew it!') are already settling in. We are right back where we were before – same issues, same positions. What is clear here, however, is that we are using each other to become conscious. We actually *want* to get caught at our games. We *want* to stop playing them and heal. And there is no better way to learn our life lessons than to be in a challenging relationship.

Of course not everybody engages in this kind of full-on drama. Some of us keep ourselves quietly tucked away in our own little worlds, not risking inviting anyone in. Or perhaps we date someone *safe*, who doesn't challenge us, who, because of his or her own fears, is complicit in maintaining a lifeless, spiritless relationship. Either way, when we don't turn on the light to see what's holding us back, our lower self has control of us.

You see, it's neither bad luck nor your *fault* that you haven't found Mr or Ms Right. You – and the people you attract – are simply drawn to people who confirm your old beliefs. But it doesn't have to stop there. Being that we are on this earth to learn and grow, time has not been wasted. In fact, you can look at it this way: you were brought to this place for the sole purpose of unveiling the great potential within you. Now it's up to you to take advantage of the moment.

> *The mind is its own place, and in itself can make heaven of hell, a hell of heaven.*
>
> —JOHN MILTON

One of the first tasks, then, is to identify the behaviors you've been using to prevent a healthy partnership. Let's take a look at some of the common ones:

Relationship-Defeating Behaviors

- Defensiveness
- Self-pity
- Fault finding
- Resentment
- Insecurity
- Codependency
- Possessiveness
- Addiction
- Victimization
- People pleasing
- Being secretive
- Passive aggressiveness
- Self-neglect, i.e., the martyr
- Trying to change someone

- Creating constant drama
- Being a control freak
- Trying to be someone you're not

Self-pity is a stance that keeps you from seeing beyond what you perceive to be unfair circumstances; by staying mired in self-pity you never have to confront your own responsibility for your situation.

Fault finding is designed to make you feel superior by diminishing your partner's confidence. Eventually he or she will tire of being criticized and leave, or worse, hang in there and take up the position of martyr.

Resentment is a festering grudge that clouds balanced perception, allowing no room for forgiveness. It becomes impossible to feel good about much in each other when resentment predominates.

Insecurity assumes that your partner will hurt you in some way and compulsively seeks assurance of approval and fidelity. This creates a dynamic where one person is needy and the other feels burdened and/or withholding.

Codependency is the entanglement of our own identity with our partner's, so that we can't act from our own personal truth.

Possessiveness gives neither person room to breathe. When we deny someone autonomy, we suffocate the relationship.

Addiction makes something other than God our Higher Power, which leaves the ego dangerously in control of the relationship.

Victimization polarizes each partner into assuming a role of separation. There is always an unspoken agreement in this sort of a relationship where one partner gets to play the all-powerful controller (usually because they feel weak and powerless inside) and the victim gets to take no responsibility for the state of their life.

People pleasing is unattractive because almost all actions are calculated for a specific response rather than being authentic. We all sense when something is false, and because we feel manipulated somehow we reject that person.

Being secretive hides our true self from a partner, making the other distrustful and suspicious.

Passive aggressiveness is impossible to deal with because of its insidious nature; we can't get a clear communication but feel anger coming at us. But if it is not owned, we can't address the problem and resolve it.

Self-neglect, i.e., the martyr attempts to lay guilt and draw pity. This polarizes the partner into being the victimizer.

Trying to change someone basically tells your partner they are not good enough.

Creating constant drama wears out both partners, exhausting the well of genuine emotion a healthy relationship draws from.

Being a control freak makes your partner feel like he or she can never do anything right, which then breeds resentment and separation.

Now comes the hard part. I want you to rate, on a scale

of 1 to 3, how much you partake in each or any of these behaviors: (1) not at all, (2) sometimes, and (3) this is your whole modus operandi. Then tally how many of each number you have. If you rated most of the patterns with a (1), you are very well adjusted! If you checked off a few (2)'s, you would do well to pay attention to potential relationship hazards. And if you chose even one (3), know that you are keeping love at a distance.

Remember, everybody has *stuff* – issues that are looking to be resolved. You're just seeing your stuff more clearly now that you have invited the healing spirit of Grace into your life. So now it should be easy to just stop being relationship defeating, right?

Well, not exactly. If only it were that easy. No, these behaviors don't give up without a bit of a fight. They're old, they're lodged deep in our psyches, and we continue to find reasons to justify their existence. We attract what we put out: 'You see, I really am a victim. Look what he did to me now!' But it takes two to keep these dances going, and somewhere along the line, you signed up for the dance. In order to stop, you have to be willing to really deal with your stuff.

You might feel a little lost for a while. And that can make you panic. We are so accustomed to believing that we are defined by our relationships (careers, etc.), that they are who we are. Until we grasp that there really is *nothing* lasting and truly fulfilling in this life other than being in touch with spirit, we'll never find a real miracle partnership.

To fall into a habit is to begin to cease to be.
                                   —MIGUEL DE UNAMUNO

Whenever we invest someone else with the power to define who we are, we inevitably come to resent them for failing to live up to the impossible task of doing what only God can do.

> When we think a partner should be healing our pain through unconditional love, they cannot help but fail because it is only God who can do that.

Anyone seeking that feeling of absolute love through another person, or a job, or having 'things,' is experiencing what I call 'God hunger.' We rage at what we cannot get and feel helpless because our soul really does know that our thirst cannot be quenched by anything other than the true connection and alignment with Spirit. We're hungry for love but we keep blocking ourselves from being nourished.

If more parents would recognize that part of their role is to mentor us in aligning with spirit, we would naturally move toward God as we grow older. But because they often don't know how to lead us down that path, we use crushes, infatuations, and then the full-blown drama of relationships to create that feeling of connection. Instead of finding ourselves, many of us lose ourselves. So now that we have at least a preliminary awareness of what we do to create obstacles to our own happiness, it's time to begin to turn things around.

WHY WE DO IT

> *Nothing determines who we will become so much as those things we choose to ignore.*
>
> —SANDOR MCNAB

We are all born with certain lessons to learn and we unconsciously create situations in our lives to help us fulfill this destiny, to help us discover our power. Certain conflicts arise in early childhood to point us toward our path. They are the fundamental building blocks for the personalities we become. They drive us to figure things out, to seek enlightenment, and to become closer to the God potential within. You see, our wounds are gifts – sometimes very, very painful ones, but always doorways we are forced through so that we can see beyond our personal limits to the grander scheme of life.

Whether we felt abandoned or in some way profoundly not cared for, the experiential memory of not getting the love and attention we needed became lodged in our Trinity Self. To survive, we developed personalities to cope with this sense of lack. To this day, whenever we experience a trauma (no matter to what degree) we go to old coping mechanisms. We hold tightly to these old ways because to give them up would mean letting go of the grasp that keeps the world familiar and 'in place.'

Take, for example, the child of an alcoholic. A child of an alcoholic parent or parents usually experiences the parent as emotionally unavailable. The child might learn that the only way to get 'positive strokes' is by cleaning up the mess the addict leaves in his wake. She might learn that the only way to feel good about herself is to always be the one to anticipate or fix whatever problems the parent isn't able to fix. This fix-it behavior, unless attended to, will usually carry over into her adult relationships. She'll either be attracted to addicts or at least to people who are as emotionally unavailable as the parent and then attempt to win him over with her extraordinary caretaking skills. And so, she keeps repeating the pattern she learned in childhood.

At the point that we recognize that these old coping behaviors don't work for us, we have a choice: we can either dig in and submerge ourselves more deeply into being frustrated and alone, or simply decide once and for all to face whatever it was that caused us so much fear and pain.

Often, as people begin this work, they tap into a profound sense of grief. Rather than pushing yourself to 'get over it' and move on, now is the time to tend to this grief. There is no more powerful step than to *feel and move through* the feelings that have been holding you hostage all your life.

This may mean crying for a week, or writhing in pain at

the helplessness you feel. Whatever comes up for you, it's so important that you just let yourself feel it and have compassion for yourself. Rest assured that I will be giving you some tools to help you dismantle your old patterns and come into your authentic self.

> Our woundedness invokes the spirit of healing, and thus the spirit of Grace.

THE ROLE OF FEAR

The root feeling that serves as an obstacle to a soulful relationship is fear. As I've explained, everything we do, say, and perceive originates either from fear or from love. If you slow down and ask yourself where you're coming from at any given moment, you'll clearly see one of the two at work. When we are fearful we create façades and personas to defend ourselves. For instance, we may act cocky and sure of ourselves, when in fact we're terrified of being seen as the insecure person with nothing to say.

It's true that when we are afraid, we are not tapped into our spiritual nature. And when we are not tapped into our spiritual nature, we are not nearly as interesting, beautiful, and magnetic as we could be. In this sense our insecurity is well founded, but as long as we continue to be guided by fear rather than love, we will never attract anyone *other* than someone who reinforces that fear. It's all self-created and self-perpetuating. We send out an unconscious or fear-based message and the Universal Mind fills the order with the perfect person to match.

So let's talk about the fears that can be guiding our lives even without our conscious awareness. There is the fear of not being enough, of being alone, of being seen for who we really are, and of course the all-too-talked-about fear of commitment. These are powerful dictators of energy, for as we hold to a thought based on fear, energy gathers around it and actually creates the very experience we're afraid of.

For instance, a commonly held belief among women is that we can't do it alone. Some of us are so afraid of being alone that we stay locked in bad relationships. But every time we make a decision such as staying with someone we really don't love because we fear the alternative, we tell the universal mind that we have no faith. That we will settle.

The desperate quality of thinking we *need* someone to take care of us only keeps away the energy of a rich relationship. Many of us succumb to a pattern of grabbiness, which, understandably, pushes people away. It's completely self-defeating. The irony here is that once we learn to be self-sufficient and fulfilled all on our own, in walks the relationship we never believed we could have. In profoundly giving up, we open ourselves to clear the way.

Our lives are like a vessel through which divine energy flows; if we don't clear the stumbling blocks that we encounter, we keep the energy of a spiritual relationship from entering.

∽

Last year, I had a client who often said to her partner, 'Please, don't ever leave me.' Even if Ingrid didn't always voice it, her plea was picked up on a subconscious level, making her boyfriend feel suffocated and wanting to get away. This had happened to Ingrid time and again, but she never connected the dots and realized she might be bringing about her own 'abandonment.'

Being a professional woman, Ingrid thought she had it all together. She was moving up the ladder and was considered by her friends and coworkers to be a very strong, secure woman. Yet the pattern of Ingrid's fear being realized by a series of boyfriends leaving her persisted. She tried to reason that her aloneness was a consequence of putting her career first, and figured it was a price she'd have to pay in order to be successful. However, being the woman who wanted it all, she wanted to find a way around this.

So she came to my workshop to deal with the issue of balancing career and love life. After doing some soul-searching exercises, Ingrid saw that her conundrum was not a matter of how to prioritize her life, but that she created an abandonment fantasy fulfillment by railing against it.

Through the clearing meditations, Ingrid realized that she was reenacting old cycles of abandonment from her father leaving her mother when she was four. She'd never really dealt with the wound, and instinctively looked for a man to prove that she was enough to keep him. It was that hurt child that spoke through the woman, the fear and insecurity always making her partner leave. The very thing Ingrid feared was what inevitably happened.

We worked on these problems by identifying exactly what her feelings about abandonment were, and the fear that motivated Ingrid's neediness. She learned to recognize the dysfunctional behavior when it arose, and took steps to reprogram her communications with men. For Ingrid, understanding why she related in such a way that scared men off was a breakthrough, in that, once understood, she could change it.

I cannot stress this enough: *We cannot exist within both places – love and fear – simultaneously.* Every moment we make a choice to come from one or the other. If we can't even look at who we are in the deepest regions of our being because of the fear of what we might discover, we are saying to the universe that we are ashamed of ourselves. If we were to choose to come from love instead, we would welcome the chance for introspection, knowing that we did the best we could.

To neutralize the energy of fear, which shows up as suspicion, doubt, or anxiety, we first have to recognize what we get out of it. What is the binding reward that keeps us isolated from our higher selves? For example, if you habitually find yourself taking care of your partner to the point where you can no longer even identify your own needs, you might ask what reward you gain from this dance. Perhaps it gives you a good excuse not to pursue your career, or allows you the comfort of playing small in the world.

If you tend not to get into relationships in the first place, you also have something to gain by not looking too deeply into yourself. Sometimes it's just plain laziness that keeps love at bay. We don't have to go on the diet, or exercise, or worry about how we've let ourselves go. All of that would mean we had enough self-esteem to take the time to care for ourselves. If we don't take care of ourselves, the message is that we are not worth caring for.

If you are alone or staying in an unfulfilling relationship, I want you to ask yourself, right now: 'What reward do I get by hanging onto these patterns of relating?'

EXERCISE: WHAT I GET OUT OF IT

In this exercise you will be identifying various negative behaviors that you engage in and looking at why you continue to do them. In the left column, I want you to list three behavioral patterns that have pretty much played out repetitively in past relationships. In the right, I want you to try to identify what you get out of each.

Remember to be compassionate with yourself. We all do the best that we know how.

BEHAVIOR	WHAT I GET OUT OF IT
Example: I play the victim.	People feel sorry for me and are nice to me.

Catching ourselves at our own game can be pretty humbling because we have to take responsibility for the fact that we've had a part in creating our current situation. Having seen what we do, we no longer have the luxury of ignorance.

Of course we can become conscious and still not change. In fact, many people, once they uncover what they've really been up to, just start carrying around a lot of guilt, embodying the belief that they don't *deserve* love. But we get nowhere by beating ourselves up and being ashamed at what we've found. That only creates self-loathing, and self-loathing simply draws to us relationships that confirm we are not lovable. No, we have to take the next step and recover our self-esteem. After all, no one can love us, truly, until we love ourselves.

To face our demons is to hearten the soul.

Some people are lucky enough to have a pretty good sense of self-esteem throughout their lives, but most of us are not so lucky. The great thing is that when we really grapple with our most challenging issues, we get the reward not only of renewed self-esteem but of the incredible pride of having taken the leap and devoted ourselves to change. Truthfully, our fears are just like bullies: when we face them, we can see that they don't have nearly the power we thought they did. When challenged, they tend to slink away.

How We Change It

The task now is to reveal your behaviors and patterns so that you can see how you've helped create your current relationship reality. Make no mistake: taking your own inventory is painful. It's difficult to face up to how much you've done wrong in your life. But if you don't, you'll just keep re-creating the same result of unfulfilling relationships.

Let's say there's a part of you that wants not to be the victim in relationships anymore. You say to yourself, 'No more bad guys!' But you still won't look at your part in the dance, thinking it's just been your bad luck to happen upon abusers. Instead of seeing that there are parts of yourself that actually enjoy people's pity, or admit that you just want to be taken care of rather than creating your own destiny, you take that anger (even disgust) out on the next partner who begins to show signs of the old.

Rather than seeing the shame that has a hold on you, you become obsessed with making the other guy wrong. You desperately want him to see your goodness – and to stop treating you so badly. But this bad treatment is only a reflection of your own self-loathing. Now you feel resentful, and your level of magnetism is scouring bottom. Ah, the games we play . . .

The old adage remains true: 'The meaning of insanity is to do the same thing over and over and expect a different result.'

No. Now it's time to ask yourself: 'Am I willing to take a good, hard look at who I am and how I've been keeping love away? Am I willing to take a risk and shift into something different?' To help you identify and let go of old, self-defeating behaviors, I've created the following six-step process.

DISSOLUTION SOLUTION

1. Identify the old, dysfunctional behavior.

2. Accept it.

3. Go through the emotions attached – i.e., grieving, raging, etc.

4. Devise a plan on how to change the behavior. You can do this by: a) catching yourself doing it; b) taking a deep breath and being willing to do things differently; c) asking for help from your Higher Power to show you

how; and d) looking at how healthy people do it and trying it on for size!

5. Make amends where necessary.

6. Forgive yourself and anyone else involved, and let it go.

It's important that you be ruthlessly honest with yourself. I'm not suggesting that it's even possible, much less desirable, to clear the slate of everything that is negative; but when we repress 'dark' feelings, they often come out kicking and screaming to get our attention, as if to say, 'Look at me, pay attention, I'm here and I'm not going away!'

Feelings such as sadness, anger, and regret are not only natural but necessary: they protect us and maintain internal boundaries. Anger, for example, is appropriate when someone hurts you or crosses a line. Sadness ritualizes someone's passing or helps us to process rejection. And regret is a way that we can go back and see where we were misguided and therefore change what we do in the future. You see, this process is not about judging your behavior, it's only about bringing it to light. Simply allowing yourself to have your 'dark' feelings loosens their grip.

I consider this step the hardest one of my seven steps. It has us making peace with our shadow selves, and to do that we have to venture into the dark corners of our psyche. But taken one small step at a time, and with an attitude of non-judgment, it is entirely manageable. And it really is the only path to the other side. As it is often said, 'The only way out is through.'

So the lesson here is to accept where you are, and to forgive yourself. Accept all the different aspects of yourself, rosy or not. Remind yourself often: You are where you are because it was the best you could do up to now.

FORGIVENESS

Let's talk a moment about what it is to forgive. Forgiveness is not the self-righteous stance of being the one who either doles out mercy or condemnation. That kind of attitude comes from our manipulative ego-minded self, which tries to maintain control through judgment. Remember, the ego self is the opposite of the God self within us, and we want to constantly be vigilant about not indulging that smaller part of ourselves. Forgiveness is, in fact, a reminder that we are all equal and it is not our place to sit in judgment of ourselves or any other human being.

Forgiving someone, yourself included, has us acknowledge that the only real thing is the love underneath the fear. Everything else was just an illusion. If someone hurt you, you are able to see that the higher part of them didn't do that, they just got caught up in their own fear. If you did something terrible to someone, you now acknowledge that the perfect, innocent part of you was being covered up by fearful perceptions. Literally, forgiveness is to see the event again, differently. To know that there is no guilt, simply growth. To let go of that kind of weight frees the soul and attracts the mate.

Mantra

I am willing to forgive and see the innocence beyond the act.

Judging others can be very seductive, but whatever it is we now judge was at some point something we accepted; after all, we have participated in every relationship we've had as consenting adults. When we keep pointing our finger at someone who has wronged us we stay invested in that unhealthy energy instead of freeing ourselves from it.

Think of the energy that is robbed by holding on to judgment's toxic residue; how can love fight its way through such a thick and murky field of energy? Indeed, the passion of the unforgiving weakens our power to magnetize.

It might also be challenging to forgive someone of a quality that you yourself might identify with on some level. If you didn't embody the very thing you hold in judgment, it wouldn't resonate with you, and therefore wouldn't be such an issue. That's why it's so important to release others, and yourself, from judgment and forgive in the deepest sense. Otherwise you'll keep unknowingly grabbing on to relationships that *click* into familiar patterns.

Let me be clear here that I'm not talking about taking responsibility for wounds that were dealt you in childhood, though those, too, can be considered painful lessons given to you so that you might learn and grow.

Once you can let go of judgment and the anger that surrounds it, the gentleness of a spiritual relationship will be waiting just beyond that veil.

When you forgive, you are actually aligning your energy with that of Grace, becoming more in tune with the God energy within, which is the great magnetic force and creator of relationships. I want to stress that I'm not only talking about forgiving people who might have hurt *you*, I'm just as strongly advising that you forgive *yourself*. Probably half of the condemnation we walk around with is doled out to us by ourselves. If you could only treat yourself with the kindness you might offer a stranger, the benefit of the doubt that you are doing the best you can, you'd be well on your way. When we forgive ourselves we remember who we are and our prayer for a great relationship is unfettered by the degenerative belief that we are not enough.

Interestingly, this process you're undertaking will not necessarily be supported by some of your friends or family; people don't always want you to change or let go of the blame game. They want camaraderie in *their* need to hang on and they need your fellowship in order to do that. It's easy to give in to the temptation of holding firm to bitter resentments and toxic thinking. The world engages in that every day. But we're striving for something great here, for the enlightened partnership, and so we have to make our way without too much regard for outside influence.

> Forgiveness is an active force, which softens the walls around the heart.

I understand how hard it is to let go of something; sometimes the only way we can survive is by compartmentalizing a painful experience by putting it in a place that we feel will keep us separated, safe from its effects. But in fact, because a thought is connected and returns to the thinker, that survival instinct may be exactly what's keeping you attached to someone or something that is continuing to hurt you.

∞

Cecelia held a great deal of anger for men in general. And, though she tried to ignore it, whenever she entered into a new relationship it always came to the surface, ruining the relationship for her. The man she was with would invariably react to her resentment, giving her more fuel for the fire. It was a vicious cycle Cecelia couldn't seem to break.

The last relationship she'd had before I met her was with a man named Jason, whom she shouldered with her fear, doubt, and resentment. Cecelia's distrust made it impossible to get close to her, so he held back in a cool reserve, because he was afraid she'd try to hurt him if he didn't. She had a prosecutorial zeal that she just couldn't keep under wraps, and she grilled Jason about everything he did and said. Eventually he couldn't take it anymore and left Cecelia, confirming yet again her beliefs about the untrustworthiness of any man's commitment.

I was able to read between the lines from what Cecelia was telling me because she herself had an intellectual understanding of her situation. She'd been to therapy and knew why she felt the way she did: Cecelia clung to the anger she had for her father's coldness, and how he was never there for her when she was a child. She also had built upon this by her history with men, which snowballed her feelings of abandonment. Cecelia was smart enough to know she'd never have a good relationship because she didn't trust a man, and that the feeling ran very, very deep.

I pointed out to Cecelia that an intellectual understanding of an issue was always helpful, but almost never enough to free you from its pattern. The case in point being that Cecelia's anger still grinded at her and ruined her relationships: her life was not set up for joy. One of the sticking points for her was that her father was still married to her mother, so Cecelia was always reminded when she went home to visit that men really don't respect women and that marriage was an inherently unhappy institution.

We needed to work on forgiveness for more than one reason. On the one hand, Cecelia loved her mother very much, and since her father was a big part of her mother's life and would always be there, she just couldn't cut him out of her life. Even if she were able to simply ignore her father, her own deep-seated feelings would remain, and the damage had been done.

Cecelia needed to forgive her father for his sins against her, whether he was asking her for it or not. It didn't matter what he wanted or needed, my concern was for Cecelia, and the best thing for her was to truly forgive him, freeing herself of anger and resentment: this would also have the effect of not pushing men away from her. When she forgave him, she found there was an energetic opening – no longer the need to project guilt onto all men. Because she didn't assume their guilt, men did not flee from her harsh judgment.

Okay, so how do we go about this process of forgiveness? There are various ways. One is to simply make the decision and hold to it. Another, and this may be more difficult, is to make amends to whomever you've hurt – including yourself. So, whether you pick up the phone to apologize for things you've done, or write a letter to let someone know you're aware of your role in the conflict, you are putting closure onto a situation that was a constant drain on your energetic force. You can forgive yourself, forgive someone else, and make amends for what you've done, but you absolutely *cannot* force amends from someone else.

When making amends it's important to consider what kind of energy you could stir up. If calling someone to make amends would hurt them, or you for that matter, it might be better to write an unsent letter, or simply talk about it with a trusted confidant. By sharing your intention of forgiveness, you deflate the force that has so long kept you from moving forward.

If you really give it a try but find that you simply cannot let go of a grudge, then ask for assistance from God, your Higher Power, that you might be released and able to one day be clear of the grudge. Sometimes we are simply not ready to take that step, but the willingness is enough to shift the energy. When we're willing to consider the possibility of forgiveness, the gesture will surely follow in due time.

Remember, part of what we are doing here is releasing ourselves from the bondage of old anger, hurt, and resentment. When we forgive, really forgive, our perception of the world changes. And as our perception shifts, new players come into our lives to support our new perspective. This is the real miracle. When we get out of our own way, the relationship appears.

What I've been asking you to do in this chapter is nothing short of cutting ties with your old, dysfunctional patterns, giving up your old identity to make space for the new. No small feat! I created the following meditation in order to honor your courage and honesty in taking this critical step. Take a moment now and try the meditation, which will help you ritualize this profound change.

CUTTING THE TIES MEDITATION

1. Sit in a meditative posture with your eyes closed and your mind open. In your inner vision, place before you the person or act you wish to forgive.

2. See the situation in its entirety, noting the intention of both parties and the wound that motivates them. Be very clear in your understanding that you both did the best that you could at the time.

3. See the attachment between you as a cord of energy and

feel the force that keeps you bonded to this person.

4. Lovingly tell them that you're going to cut the ties, and that you forgive all that has transpired, knowing that it was all an illusion that the ego created out of fear.

5. In your imagination produce a pair of golden scissors and, holding the cord, sever the connection. Watch how that person fades from sight, taking their energy with them.

6. Physically experience pushing the severed cord that still is dangling outside of you back into your own body.

7. Release this person or incident with love and feel the energy regenerating your Trinity Self.

8. Breathe deeply as you let the newfound peace seep into every fiber of your being. And quietly open your eyes and feel the sense of release.

As they say in physics, nature abhors a vacuum. So once you get rid of the old stuff there is room for a new set of circumstances; the space that you made by forgiving will be filled by the new energy of potential.

It's natural that we cling to old formats in our lives; it's what we have witnessed, been taught, and become comfortable with. For a new relationship to have the space to enter, your energy cannot be clouded by beliefs that you're not someone lucky enough or deserving of having a partner who loves you in the way you want to be loved. Clearing old grudges is one of the best ways I know to becoming magnetic to a loving relationship.

The process of clearing the blocks is important because there is a direct correlation between the weakness in ourselves and the weakness that will show up in a relationship. A relationship (or lack thereof) simply reflects who we are and what we believe we deserve on the deepest level.

As we go about clearing grudges and freeing ourselves up for healthy relationships, we can be tempted to sabotage the good and go backwards, but we have to keep the faith that we are becoming our True Self, the one that has always been our potential.

> *We must embrace struggle. Every living thing conforms to it. Everything in nature grows and struggles in its own way, establishing its own identity, insisting on it at all cost, against all resistance.*
> —RAINER MARIA RILKE

Through the work you've done in this chapter, you have unsuppressed blocked energy, which will in turn decompress your spirit, opening the door for a great relationship to breathe and thrive. Part of the healing is in experiencing the pain that comes up as you go through this process of purification. Know that it is necessary but will pass. You might experience depression, anxiety, loneliness, and you might want to act out in other ways (overeating, etc.). If you do, it is time to find fellowship and support. Do things for yourself that bring comfort: go to funny movies, get massages, attend inspiring lectures, hang out with friends.

This period of purification will last as long as you need it to. Sometimes you really need time to mourn the loss of your old identity and it takes months, and sometimes it's just a matter of days. In the next step we'll be discussing what it means to create a new identity and how to go about forging a new, more authentic self. But for now, allow yourself whatever time it takes to cleanse and purify any darkness that has held you back. Look at the issues, but don't dwell on them.

Do what you can at your own pace and take breaks when you need to. Though things can happen in an instant, be patient with your progress; as they say in the Twelve-Step program of AA, 'Progress, not perfection.'

Seven Everyday Tips to Assist in Step 4, Clearing the Way:

1. Call someone you've wronged and make amends.

2. Clean out your closets as a symbol of purifying your internal energy.

3. Do a cleansing diet to detoxify the body.

4. When you're in the shower, visualize all the old patterns being washed away with the water.

5. Give up a bad habit – i.e., smoking, eating sugar, biting your nails, etc.

6. If there is a particular situation that needs your attention, commit to dealing with it within three days. Address it within that time, and then let it go.

7. See a cleric or spiritual counselor and formally ask for forgiveness to ritualize this process.

Source the Miracle

... the moment one definitely commits oneself, then Providence moves too. A whole stream of events issues from the decision, raising in one's favor all manner of unforeseen incidents, meetings and material assistance, which no man could have dreamt would have come his way. I learned a deep respect for one of Goethe's couplets:

'Whatever you can do or dream you can, begin it.
Boldness has genius, power and magic in it.'

— W. H. MURRAY

In Step 4, we dug pretty deep into your motivations to understand the internal mechanisms at work, and now you may be feeling rather raw. Just allow whatever it is you are feeling and know that in this next step you will start reaping the rewards. All the work you've been doing is clearing the way for the emergence of your highest, most magnetic self. Now let's help you get into that mind-set from which the miracle of a wonderful relationship will naturally flow.

We are told by science that we humans use only a fraction of our actual brain capacity, and that we have not even begun to access or understand all that our brains are capable of. Many researchers are just now finding evidence that the human brain is not just a housing for cognitive functions but is actually wired to perceive of and connect with a metaphysical reality that is perhaps what we know of as God. Just think of the miracles we could manifest if we could develop that circuitry that connects the mystical and the earthly.

As quantum mechanics shows in experiments with particles at the edge of our perception, the observer alters the reality of the observed just by the act of witnessing. We only know that something actually is so because of the trail it leaves behind, and we are connected to that trail of 'reflections' by our testimonial of it: what we perceive, whether real to anyone else or not, is the trail that becomes the story of our life.

When we think something, in an instant our reality mirrors that thought. It's not to say that we think of gummy bears and gummy bears appear; but that we think of them and our mouth waters, our stomach rumbles, and we crave them. A whole string of reactions comes from that simple thought: you might go out and get them, or feel guilty after eating them, or whatever. But you threw the stone (thought) into the water (possibility) and it forever changed that very moment (reality). We do create our reality. So with this concept in mind, we can enter in to a new possibility of creating love in our lives.

We are what we think. All that we are arises with our
thoughts. With our thoughts we make the world.

—BUDDHA

You can actually bring about the relationship you seek, and the love you want to experience, by magnetizing the ideal which is seeded in your subconscious mind. The power to do so already exists within you; what you need to do is shape your desire and dream, give it form and essence, and then nourish it with all of your emotion and intention. The purpose of this step is to help bring that dream into form.

We generate the circumstances of our lives with our deeply held beliefs and the emotional responses to every thought, action, and situation that arises. So to find ourselves in a great relationship, we have to first imagine it. We have to feel it in our bones, know it in every cell of our being: because to have something manifest in the outside world, it must first reside within.

Our inner world is like a laboratory that is constantly mixing our beliefs with the confirmations that come our way from everyday experience. This constantly changing energy within will be reflected in the conditions of our lives.

Mantra

In each moment my life is created new.

What is decided upon in our subconscious seeks verification in the exterior world. This happens from moment to moment, never ending. And with each new experience, our creative energy is adjusted accordingly. It is for this reason that we must be vigilant with the messages we internalize: with every action and reaction, every assumption and every deeply held belief, we are programming our lives. So if we want to become conductors of a loving relationship, we have to fill our minds with thoughts of love and our bodies with the impulses of love.

> What we perceive the world to be is what our world becomes.

We may not have the power to choose *all* the elements of our existence (that's left up to God, or chance, or however you look at the unknowable), but we do have the power, in every moment, to perceive them with love or from fear. Let's face it, we're all dealt a particular hand in this life, but how we interact with it is what creates our own personal reality. And from that interaction we set our story in motion. So, let's begin this task of creating a transformation in your love life by conditioning your subconscious mind to the experience of being in a wonderful relationship.

SENSORY IMAGING

If I were to tell you right now that you could be with a (single) Mel Gibson type if you wanted to, you probably wouldn't believe me because the idea is too foreign. What's more is that, should he come along, your inner truth of what is possible might well hinder the opportunity or actually reject the person out of fear and uncertainty. Too good to be true would be true to you.

But think of it this way: If you spent some time letting your psyche get comfortable with his essence, his qualities, you might feel quite secure with the person who shows up, even with all his 'stuff' that at one time would have intimidated you. I'm not talking about obsessing or fantasizing in the negative sense – that energy is lodged in a disassociation with reality – but of really getting comfortable with the fundamental nature of that *sort* of man. The same idea goes for being able to resonate with a fabulously healthy and loving relationship. If you can't be comfortable with how that feels inside, then you're not going to manifest it.

So how do you get comfortable? You use your imagination. You close your eyes, go within, and create a new world. In your mind you can have things exactly as you want, creating the finest scenario you can imagine and then interacting with it: become part of it and let it become part of you. You literally dream something and then settle yourself into letting that dream completely overtake you.

Mantra

I am in utter synchronicity with life's highest possibilities.

If you're not using your core energy with the intention of shifting your potential, you are passively directing all your creative output to the old habitual stuff. Our thoughts, our focus, have to go somewhere, so if we don't consciously bring them to the image we wish to manifest, all of that energy will go right into making reappear the scenarios we so wanted to leave behind. One way or the other our attention supports and grows whatever it focuses on, so now is the time to really decide on and make happen the vision of your perfect mate.

∞

Meet my friend Karen. Karen is a good example of someone who did not know how to focus and direct her creative energy, leaving it to go wherever it would. An interior designer, Karen was accustomed to using her imagination for the practical matter of envisioning what was possible before it was actually evident. But, oddly enough, she never thought to direct the energy she'd put into making a home warm and beautiful toward finding the right man.

Having divorced when she was in her twenties, Karen went through a succession of relationships, always hoping afterward that she'd meet the right man eventually. But for one reason or another it never happened and, as she approached forty-five, Karen became despondent that she'd end up growing old alone.

As we looked into her problem a few things became clear. Karen was, in fact, putting a lot of thought into the kind of man she wanted. At first glance this might have seemed like the right thing to do, but upon further inquiry I found that the way she was thinking about her relationships had a lot to do with why they never worked out.

Apparently Karen couldn't help but see herself in scenarios that were unhealthy; it was all she ever knew. Her marriage had been acrimonious and ended badly when her husband walked out one day without warning, and most of her relationships that followed quit in the same sort of drama. She would foresee falling for a man, getting involved, counting on him, and then having everything dissolve and being abandoned. So, as much as she thought she was focusing on the ideal, she was really giving her energy to what she feared would happen instead.

Karen was visualizing, without realizing it, a negative scenario that became more 'true' with each confirmation in real life. She was well acquainted with her fears and insecurities and would obsess on them in detail while trying to fantasize her perfect man. She inadvertently painted a picture of the kind of man who would do exactly what she didn't want to happen. Since this was such a powerful sensory image in her psyche, Karen always inadvertently responded when she met a man who possessed these traits: she thought her feeling of recognition was chemistry and that he might be The One, but it was really just her deep-seated fears and visions saying 'Yes, he is The One, the same one.' And so the scenario would play out again, exactly as her inner vision imagined it to.

I reminded Karen that she had an alternative. She had the choice to use her formidable imagination to help her in a positive way. But what she had to do was consciously redirect all her senses toward meeting the right kind of man for her. She had to feel his essence seep into her, replacing the haunting images from her history.

Karen took steps to redirect her energy, using all of her capability. She first thought deeply and realistically about the traits the right man would actually have, and then she began to visualize him as a living being. She imagined how he would act toward her, what he'd say and do, and how she'd act toward him.

After honing this image and meditating on the fact that what was important was his essence and not an exact physical match, Karen released her vision to the outside world at large, letting it live in her periphery. Not long after that, in an unexpected way, she met George, who seemed to embody a different kind of partner than Karen had experienced before, and this time her psyche was able to recognize it, and she responded. Karen had created a new comfort zone, which George fit in nicely.

Think of that feeling you have when you meet someone and you feel you've known him or her all your life. It's as if his or her essence has been floating around in the periphery of your consciousness and when you meet him or her you think, 'Oh right, yes. You.' It's this sort of recognition of our soul's partner that we are going to work on bringing closer to the surface.

Ask yourself now what your perfect partner would be like. Think about age, build, coloring. And then think about the qualities this person embodies and the character he or she has earned. Let yourself drift and fantasize while a picture begins to take shape. You want to note in your mind the things that would make this person a perfect match, while at the same time leaving enough room for him or her to have the spontaneity of a living being. Listen to what the person might be saying to you.

Now ask yourself, would you feel comfortable on a date with the person you've envisioned? Spending a life with him or her? If you aren't entirely confident that this is a good match, your psyche will reject the person with one form or another of sabotage when he or she comes along. The idea is to get yourself finely attuned to this 'person's' essence, so that when he or she does appear, you're perfectly comfortable. It is as if you've known the person all along – and you have!

> We all have an internal switch, which gauges who fits with us at any given time, so the idea is to raise its accuracy.

I don't know about you, but if I'd met my perfect guy ten years ago, I would have been stricken with the terror of 'not being good enough' or not knowing how to be with him and somehow (if he didn't reject me first) I would have sabotaged the relationship. We have to be ready to truly receive what we ask for.

If you've had a lifetime of disappointing relationships, the grooves of those experiences are so deeply cut into your psyche that you literally have to form *new* paths of thinking, perceiving, and feeling that will then settle into your cellular chemistry. The best way I know to do that is through sensory imaging, where you draw from your creative mind images of what you wish to invoke in the real world. In this way you get used to *feeling* and *seeing* something different, so that when that special someone crosses your path you will be ready and available, and click with them.

> *Reality can be beaten with enough imagination.*
> —ANONYMOUS

What is very important to understand before beginning the process of sensory imaging is that there is a vast difference between *wanting* a relationship and *needing* one. To want a relationship implies that you are adding to your life – expanding the love. Needing one implies desperation – that, as it is now, your life is not enough. Saying that you *need* something informs the universal mind that who and what you are is insufficient, which then gathers more evidence in the form of unsatisfying relationships to confirm that lack. Wanting has power, needing does not. So, take a moment and try shifting from a place of need to a place of want:

EXAMPLE:

Go from: 'I need to meet someone soon because I'm getting older.'

To: 'I want to be in a relationship so that I can experience more than I already have.'

Even physically, the body is stronger when a statement is powerfully based in sincere, deep desire rather than a weak and whiny need. Try this: put your hand in a fist and say out loud, 'I need this relationship' while a friend pushes down on it. Then do the same thing but instead say, 'I want this relationship.' Feel the difference in your strength? We are literally more powerful when we come from healthy *desire* rather than the unhealthy stance of *not having enough*.

Sensory Imaging is a technique that uses all the different senses to assemble a living experience in our imagination. The idea is to create a well-rounded world that we can then, in our minds, inhabit. If we are able to use as much of ourselves (and by that I mean to really breathe in and experience the fullness of what we are imagining) as we give to our daily routines, we can create a potent sphere of attraction with enough gravity to draw to us verification from the world around us.

EXERCISE: INTRODUCING YOUR SOUL MATE

Let's start the Sensory Imaging process by having you begin to feel the presence of your soul mate. The idea here is to give him or her a more definitive form. You're going to begin breaking new ground in the untapped regions of your creative mind, so gear up for a shift in your awareness.

1. Retreat to your sanctuary, get comfortable either sitting or lying down.

2. With your eyes closed, relax your entire body.

3. Pay close attention to your breath, letting it lead you to a sacred meeting place in your mind where you feel able to freely express your innermost self.

4. With each breath you take picture a translucent mist surrounding you in your vision. See it becoming thinner and thinner.

5. Imagine a figure beginning to emerge from the mist.

6. Without impressing upon the image any judgment or desire, allow the person to become clearer to you. You need not force details, just allow the essence of this person to begin to take physical form.

7. Let the feeling of 'ah, this person does exist!' sink into your psyche.

8. Feel his or her presence around you, making contact.

9. Let your body now relax into the comfort of knowing that your partner is near. Feel each and every cell alighting to the knowledge that you have found each other.

10. Breathe deeply ten more times, adjusting to the idea that your time has come to find yourself in the perfect relationship.

11. Slowly open your eyes, stretch out, and stay with this feeling.

Notice how there is already a shift in your energy, and lightness in your attitude. It's as if you can rest because you know that that person does indeed exist, and you're draw-ing nearer to him or her. Sometimes just the *knowingness* alone is enough to magnetize your partner; it is in this state of confidence that any desperation or anxiety or doubt falls away. If you have ever noticed someone at a party or a dinner who is just completely relaxed and happy, you can see that he or she has no problem attracting and meeting people. They don't have to *try*. By their confidence they are magnetic. So relax in this newfound feeling of sureness and go back to this meditation from time to time to remind yourself of the journey you are undertaking.

Mantra

> *I feel the presence of my soulmate and rest with*
> *the knowledge of his/her approach.*

Whether aware of it or not, we are constantly creating scenarios and choosing our life's stage. By obsessing on someone, worrying over what might or might not happen, or neurotically going over everything that's ever hurt us, we make a picture of reality within ourselves that cannot help but find its mirror image in our outer lives. If we anticipate something, our mind begins to map out a plan for what to expect and how to respond, and then prepares to move us into the experience, co-creating that very scenario merely by its readiness to interact. Ah yes, the self-fulfilling prophecy indeed!

> *Imagination is the beginning of creation. You imagine*
> *what you desire; you will what you imagine; and at*
> *last you create what you will.*
>
> —GEORGE BERNARD SHAW

By using sensory imaging you are mapping out your potential experiences by creating an internal blueprint. That future will have to fit into this basic structure if you are going to click with it. That's the catch: the blueprint is a critical faculty in the art of manifesting. You have to have a clear picture of what you really want or you'll end up missing it even if it comes along. It's nearly impossible to have something other than the internal vision you deeply, if not subconsciously, expect. The great news is you can take up the inventive paint and canvas in your imagination and make it look any way you want.

The idea behind using your multisensory perception to make the image of what you want 'live' is that the more you *really can experience* what you envision, the more powerful its quality of attraction. The more real it feels, the more straightforward the blueprint directs the subconscious energy. Picture the subconscious as an untamed, pulsing field of energy containing all your issues, motivations, and memories, and it is RUNNING YOUR LIFE! It is temperamental, moody, and ever adjusting in order to make sense of things, so it's important to give it something healthy to latch onto. Like a child needs discipline to grow and feel safe, so does the subconscious need the structure of the Internal Blueprint to invite the various energies of relationship into your life in a healthy way.

EXERCISE: CREATING AN INTERNAL BLUEPRINT FOR A RELATIONSHIP

1. Picture yourself as your most powerful and highest self. Place that image in the backdrop of a fulfilling life – complete with friends, creativity, and comfort.

2. Then see your ideal partner (who began to emerge in the earlier meditation) thriving in his or her life.

3. Imagine the two of you meeting and connecting.

4. See how perfectly the two worlds merge. Watch how easily it all comes together.

Hold this map in your mind as a guiding influence to harness all unforeseen events and happenings. Let it settle deeply into your subconscious mind so that all the free-flowing energy is harnessed and directed. Remember, you are training the subconscious mind to support and magnetize whoever (and whatever) it is you wish to manifest.

With sensory imaging you are participating in the dress rehearsal for being with your perfect partner. You can see it and feel it and know what it's like to your core, being happily and healthfully in love. Give your Trinity Self – body, mind, and spirit – the feeling and *experience* of love, and it will magnetize love.

The wonderful thing about imaging is that the image you create becomes so real that you drop any fear of not finding someone because he or she already exists inside you. Once that fear is dropped and you are blueprinted for partnership, it's just a matter of time before the man/woman will appear.

By changing on the inside, your physical *vibrations* change: sounds a little out there maybe, I know, but there's no better way to say it. Behold the person you've become:

how you carry yourself; what your eyes say; how you embody the soul who knows and experiences love.

Your body, your expressions, your very energy begins to take the posture of one who is in a great relationship. Thus your impulses are naturally shifted to conform to this new truth – you respond to the things that support the vision. Because you think and feel differently, you demonstrate your energy differently. You are reworking your belief system because those adjusted impulses bring forth adjusted experience. You're being shown – proven to – that 'this is the way it is.' And so the universal mind mirrors to you this newfound power and confidence by supplying the real, actualized relationship you've created.

EXERCISE: FEEL THE PRESENCE OF YOUR SOUL MATE

Now you're going to use the power of your creative mind to transform the energy that emanates from you and draws to you that which you desire. Again, because you will magnetize to you what feels right and comfortable, you want to experience in every fiber of your being what it's like to be in a great relationship. Remember, you're not just visualizing, you are employing your full multisensory energy.

You may want to read this through first so that you can close your eyes, or tape it so that you are guided through the experience. I also have twenty-minute CDs available (you'll find ordering information at the back of the book) for use in this process. First, use the Basic Grounding

Meditation you learned in Step 1 (page 24) to relax your entire body. And then . . .

With your eyes closed and your mind open, imagine yourself now meeting the person with whom you fall deeply in love. Slowly let the awareness of love take you over, melt ever more deeply into the image of being with your love. Breathe in the awakening, and exhale the excitement. Imagine where you are as this occurs: take in the surroundings. What is the weather like? What time of day is it? Notice how this person looks at you with complete recognition. Picture the two of you smiling, touching, and connecting. Let yourself go and let yourself go further. If you feel blocked or uninspired, just relax, and continue to invite in the image. Now let the scenario progress in time. How are you sharing your lives? What do you enjoy doing together? What is your home like: your conversations, your friends, and your vacations? Fill your mind with images that imprint a strong feeling of being happy in this relationship. Take your time here, let the scene develop and expand. Hear people telling you how they admire what you have and that they want to know your secret. See yourself surrounded by people who support and enjoy you as a couple.

Breathe all of this in and experience the satisfaction in every cell of your body. Notice your posture, your expression, and the sound of your voice in the image, and allow your body to take in and remember all the physicalities of this beautiful partnership. Feel this energy settle into your cellular imprint.

Add color to the image: bright yellow, deep purple, vibrant red. See the color of your hands, your partner's eyes. Now begin to hear sound: perhaps laughter, the quiet tones of relaxed conversation, birds chirping, the sound of the ocean. Breathe into it, absorb it.

In your ideal world fill this sensory experience with as many details and levels as you can. Smell dinner cooking, the roses outside . . . What is the taste in your mouth after kissing, the tingling on your fingertips when you're holding hands? Take the time to luxuriate in this blissful world of a loving relationship, adding as many details as you can.

Now, in your vision, as happy and fulfilled as you are, increase the volume! Add even more passion. Intensify all of your senses and infuse it with the Grace of that golden light which has created all the good. Feel yourself smile. Feel the celebration of your soul finding its mate. And then when you feel like you've taken it as far as you can, feel the snap of completion and lock it into your Trinity Self. And then take a deep breath, slowly opening your eyes. Stay where you are for a few minutes and let the shift settle into you.

An internal shift has occurred; let it resonate within you. This is what you were meant to feel, who you were meant to be. This meditation is, indeed, the map to your soul mate.

Let yourself drift in and out of this sensory image throughout the day. I suggest doing this particular meditation two times a day, for twenty minutes, for thirty days. It may sound like a lot, but considering that it took a lifetime to get where you are now, it only makes sense that it would take a bit of commitment to reprogram yourself. This is not to say you *can't* shift in an instant because you *can*, but usually the psyche needs to be ushered into this new state of being gently, patiently, and consistently. It is for this reason that we nurture the visualization regularly: hold the image firmly in the power structure between your solar plexus and brain, and then let it settle in to you. What is growing within you is already radiating outward to connect with its counterpart in the real world.

Having such an activated vision creates synchronicity in your life: suddenly you run right into who you need to meet, a superb idea presents itself, an opportunity pops up out of nowhere. Everything seems to happen so easily, almost as if by magic: you are in the Miracle Zone! Your authentic beliefs and expectations, focused by your imagination, draw to you the miracle of a great partnership. The actual *way* it unfolds is not up to you, that's God's business, so just dwell on your good feeling and the reality will present itself to further that feeling. Energy always expands on itself.

If you find that you're feeling doubtful or unsure, ask that Grace lift you into faith, and you might be shifted by God's great force and strengthened by proof of that shift. But always, when you imagine consciously, trust that the vision is on its way.

When I'm doing my own sensory imaging, it's at this point that I employ a little trick if I need to. So that I don't find myself completely living in the clouds, I shift my desire, the image, into my peripheral vision. That way I'm not too single-minded or overworked in my psychic energy. I let it settle just on the periphery of my attention. In this way, what I wish to manifest is always in my mind, but at the edge of consciousness so I can authentically experience life. Something else you can do when you feel a little stuck is to ask your Higher Power to guide you through any tough spots that arise. It might be hard to conjure up something you have no experience with – so ask for the assistance of Grace to show the way to your heart's desire. You may still be learning what you want and what you'll feel comfortable with, and that is just fine. Take your time and enjoy the journey!

Mantra

As my soul stretches, so does the scope of my potential relationship.

After doing your sensory imaging for three days, complete these sentences:

I can have this because_____

I will meet him/her because_____

It benefits the world to meet this person because

_____

You want to continue taking into consideration all three aspects of your Trinity Self. Sometimes the intellect will rail against believing this is possible because the ego sneaks in and tries to pull us back to who we were. So honor that part of you and give the intellect reason to support the vision: argue your case. Find logic to support it, and literally convince yourself that you are very much in line for a miracle to occur.

From Concept to Reality

I hope you've been saying the mantras sprinkled throughout the book. If you have, you probably have an intuitive sense of their power. They work only when you deeply embrace the truth of the words. If you repeat them in a hollow way, they are just empty phrases, and unable to affect energy. To harness their power, say them slowly and carefully, digesting the meaning and gravity behind the words.

By saying mantras throughout the day you are literally rearranging patterns of thoughts, which, based on your faith in them, can rearrange your life. You might say this is the ultimate leap of faith! Regardless of how life looks right now, you are affirming the *potential*. Mantras are not about instant magic, but about signing up for what is possible.

Think of all the negative messages we receive and repeat throughout our lives about things being difficult or not being lucky or deserving more but not getting it. For years our subconscious has been taking in and processing these negative mantras, so by sheer mathematics we need to apply an awful lot of counteractive messages.

Live out of your imagination, not your history.
—STEPHEN COVEY

Even casual, off-handed statements such as 'you'll be the death of me' or 'I'm such a loser' weigh heavily in our subconscious programming and must be avoided during this process of reprogramming. Each nerve, muscle, bone, and tissue in our body hears the message and responds accordingly, so to be conscious and deliberate about what you think punctuates the shift in energy that is your transformation. If you're surrounded by people who just will not change their messages of who you are, can't see you as any different than their historical viewpoint, then try to carve out a space away from them, and don't let their thoughts invade when they're around. People are comfortable with their projections and it's not really our place to change them. And remember, water seeks its own level, so pay attention to the subtext of all your interactions with people.

The basis of all love relationships is a fundamental belief that love can override anything. We literally raise our consciousness, and therefore our prospects, by holding and contemplating thoughts of love.

So start with yourself: override the old patterns with new mantras, messages, and beliefs of love. There is great power behind the word, especially when we have emotional conviction backing it up. We can't force a belief or coerce a new thought system, but we can find support for our mantras by our intellect and by faith. The intention to *have it be so* is really all that we need. For instance, you might try saying, '*I am in Love!*,' putting your energy there in such a concentrated way calls forth the experience to confirm it. From such statements certain impulses and intimations are mobilized to draw you closer to the actual experience.

Whatever it is you deeply believe in, the subconscious will reach out and match with an experience. Through daily mantras and Sensory Imaging, you transcend your present situation by flashing on a fresh glimpse of how things *can be*. Your higher mind makes a decision, and all of the Trinity Self embraces the truth of it.

It's important to distinguish between a positive affirmation and a lie. Saying 'I am in Love' even if you're not presently in a relationship isn't lying, it just means you are enjoying the blissful feeling (if even for a moment) of being in love.

Remember, though, that affirmations of what you want must be within the context of what's good for everyone involved. So let seep into your work the intention of everything unfolding in the highest and most evolved way.

Shelly pretty much knew just what kind of relationship she wanted, and what kind of man would be the perfect fit. She had been practicing different visualization techniques for a while, but had yet to manifest what she saw. When we spoke, Shelly expressed a great deal of frustration at not yet having been able to draw to her who she felt would make her life rich and happy, and feared that she was losing faith. But the truth was that Shelly just needed to take it a bit farther.

Already being involved with Chester made her situation a little more complicated, but Shelly was undaunted. She had been trying, since she pictured her ideal man so well, to squeeze Chester into that image. She was afraid to let him go because he seemed to be the best she could do. But it wasn't to be; Shelly knew she didn't really love Chester for who he was and that he was feeling like a consolation prize. The fact was, if she was always imagining what life would be like 'if only' she was with the right man, Shelly obviously didn't really love Chester and he deserved better than that.

So the first, although easy in concept but harder in practice, thing that had to happen was that she had to let Chester go. In order for the man to appear, Shelly had to have the firm conviction that her vision was on its way, and that she could testify to her faith by living as if it were already so. Shelly was able to do this after putting into practice some of the techniques discussed in previous chapters. Though nervous about being unattached, Shelly also felt exuberant at the thought of the possibilities that now lay before her.

Now that she was in the clear with Chester out of the picture, Shelly had to make real what she had going on in her mind. I'd coached her to get comfortable with the reality of her ideal relationship and that she could do this not just by picturing herself in the ideal relationship but living as if she had already received the miracle. Shelly needed to become the woman who exuded the confidence of being in love. She went to dinner in restaurants that she dreamed of going to with her partner, took long walks in the park, went to movies she wanted to share. At first she felt a little silly doing these things by herself, but soon came to find a kind of familiarity in them, knowing that she was drawing closer to her ideal mate. Ironically, even though she felt him 'approaching,' she was for the first time in her life quite content to be alone.

One day while Shelly was having dinner at her favorite 'ideal' restaurant, she happened to be sitting next to a man who'd been stood up by his date. Her first thought was that the woman must have been a complete fool to blow off a guy like that. He seemed to be taking it in good humor and happened to catch her eye, holding up his hands in mock helplessness when he did. Something about the way he did this clicked with Shelly and she laughed, asking if he wanted to join her.

Ryan told me that what he immediately loved about Shelly was that she was so confident and self-possessed. He was completely enchanted by the woman who seemed to be so contented with her life and played no games. Needless to say Shelly and Ryan became, and remain, quite the item.

We can counteract the force of what has made our lives loveless by replacing negative messages with loving ones – we need only hold to the commitment of transformation. If you start feeling doubtful and your old reasoning gets in the way, remember to maintain the stance of being *miracle minded*. Things can change in an instant – get out of your own way and stay open to the possibilities of love finding you no matter what. Your doubt is normal, so don't judge yourself for it; notice it, keep with the program, and let it go. Don't force anything, just keep getting lost – or found, really – in your sensory imaging. The world you create there will eventually squeeze out the world you worry about.

When we act as if we are already the people we dream to be, life lends itself to support that testament of faith. Think of the times when you have felt most attractive: it's when you just don't care about *finding the one* or *making it happen*. You're just deeply contented with life, as if you already have all that you need. And so you do.

Seven Everyday Tips to Assist Step 5, Sourcing the Miracle

1. Close your eyes, and say the word YES and let it resonate throughout your body.

2. Take yourself out on the ideal date.

3. Plant a tree and let it be the symbol of your developing ideal.

4. Imagine that you have a teacher guiding you, and whenever you feel stuck, ask for insight and strength.

5. Take an action that you would normally do only if you were in a relationship, such as keeping fresh flowers on the kitchen table or buying sexy lingerie.

6. Launch a creative project (painting, writing, dancing, etc.) in order to get the creative transformation energy flowing.

7. Notice how others you admire do things, and emulate them.

STEP 6

Find and Express Gratitude

Gratitude is merely the secret hope of further favors.
—FRANÇOIS DE LA ROCHEFOUCAULD

Now that we've established that *everything is energy*, you can see that your every thought and action, perception and reaction, contributes to who you are and what you attract in the world. When we talk about the power of thought in manifesting what we desire, I think of skiing: just think of turning right and your foot makes a slight adjustment, causing your whole body to follow that cue. In the same way, when we focus on the good that we already have in our lives, our energy takes the cue and moves toward that source of good. And since energy seeks its own level, it will find more things to *be* grateful for.

The idea of employing gratitude as part of your 'miracle strategy' lies in using what is *already* good in your life to seed more of that same (and even better) energy. Giving thanks whenever gifts present themselves simply encourages you toward your higher good. Gratitude is especially important when things are tough. By focusing on the good that is present, your energy goes to abundance rather than the scarcity you might otherwise obsess on.

> Gratitude makes us peaceful; it helps us to live in the moment.

When we turn our attention to the things that we are thankful for, a peaceful feeling naturally comes over us, as if we know we're being taken care of. It feels so good that we want to spread it around. So what do we do? We find ways to give back; we become kind and generous ourselves. Then the people around us, touched by our generosity, want to spread it around, too, and they become generous. See how it all unfolds?

And because we're not 'hanging on' to that which felt so good, we're paying it forward so we've got a cleared space for new experiences to come in.

True thanksgiving means that we need to thank God for what He has done for us, and not to tell Him what we have done for Him.

—GEORGE R. HENDRICK

In this chapter we'll be concentrating on cultivating this feeling of gratitude, so that the energy all around you gets behind creating situations that you can be grateful for. You might think that this would be the simplest step, as gratitude seems so undemanding, such a joyful undertaking, in fact. But finding and expressing gratitude can sometimes be the most challenging thing to carry out. Maybe because things just feel too awful at the moment or maybe, just by our nature, we take things for granted and forget to give thanks. But if gratitude isn't present to keep the flow going, things get stuck. The energy gets blocked. We literally cannot expect to draw more good experiences into our lives if we don't express gratitude for what we already have. So let's see how we might cultivate gratitude.

> *Gratitude is the heart's memory.*
> —FRENCH PROVERB

Of course no one reaches adulthood with only pleasant experiences and gifts to be grateful for. I think it's safe to assume that we've all had our share of tough times. When we're going through something particularly difficult, it can be awfully hard to feel grateful, hard to imagine that the experience will benefit us in some way. But we can usually look back in hindsight and find the gift that came enfolded in the struggle. Just as we discussed in Step 4 in regard to self-esteem, it is often these hard-won victories of the spirit of which we are most proud. Let me give you the example from my own life.

MY STORY

Over the years, I've been in my share of relationships – some of them good but most of them unfulfilling. At my very lowest, I got involved with an abusive man. Before the relationship ended, I had lost nearly all my self-esteem.

I met him after my modeling career had peaked. I was feeling excited about what the next stage in life held for me, having spent years working on myself spiritually. (One of the ways I would pass the time on location, waiting to shoot, was reading about various theologies and philosophies, and I felt ready to put to use some of the ideas that were coming together in my mind.) It's amazing how easily our finest plans can be shattered when the perfect reflection of all our dark fears shows up in the name of passion and attraction.

Peter (not his real name) was not classically handsome but there was something about him that just made my knees weak. He keyed into something significant in me – little did I know, at the time, it was my insecurity. We started dating and I fell madly in love with him, for reasons I now know were addictive and unhealthy. Peter wined and dined me, just long enough to get my guard down to become fully emotionally dependent on him, and then he gradually and insidiously tore down every bit of strength I had.

It started off with little things, such as telling me what to wear because he didn't really like my style, or looking blankly at me when I shared with him things that were important to me. Then he started cheating. When I found out about it he would deny it and tell me I was crazy, until I began to believe that maybe I was. Until, that is, I caught him again. And again.

By this point we were two years into the relationship and I had too much invested in it (I thought) to just walk away. Instead, I was hell-bent on figuring out why he found me so lacking that he had to go out and be with other women. I was attractive enough to have been a model, smart enough to have had articles published, and warm enough to have a lot of friends – but still . . . I wasn't enough. I couldn't have been, right? Otherwise he wouldn't have gone elsewhere.

So I hung in there, trying to prove to Peter that I was indeed committed to making him happy (his way of keeping me on my toes was to constantly tell me that I wasn't acting like I liked him), but really I think I just desperately needed my self-worth to be validated by him. So onward we went deeper into that dance of dysfunction – each of us reflecting back to the other our most deeply held fears: I, who was not enough, and he who seemed to fear he'd always be abandoned.

The relationship spiraled down to the point that I could not be with Peter without being drunk. Peter started out by shoving me when he felt frustrated, just sort of pushing me around, and then graduated to punching and kicking me if I said no to any of his sexual whims.

By now I had lost twenty pounds (he liked his women thin) and was unable to model anymore. The sparkle in my eye was gone and I became just another girl in an abusive relationship. The money I had saved was soon spent because I'd bought clothes I thought would seduce him, and spent the rest on trying to pull my own weight to prove that I didn't need his money. Toward the end of our relationship he nicknamed me 'rodent' and I actually condoned his affairs in an attempt to keep him happy.

One night Peter had hurt me so badly, and looked so mean, I thought he might want to kill me, so I pretended to faint, hoping he'd leave me alone. In my faked un-consciousness I heard him spit on me; I didn't move as it dripped down the side of my face. With his foot he shoved me around to make sure I was really out and mumbled a few obscenities before he left the house – probably to drum up another date for his ruined night. I just lay there on the cold marble floor and cried. Cried for my lost innocence, cried for my pathetic place in life. Cried for my fear of not knowing how to pick myself up and move on. And cried because I could not fix this mess.

Over the duration of time that I was with Peter, most of my friends stopped calling because they couldn't bear to witness my demise. My health had gotten quite fragile with my steady diet of alcohol, nicotine, and high anxiety. And my bank account was getting dangerously close to zero. My family watched helplessly, not really knowing the full extent of the dysfunction, often asking, 'Why don't you just leave?' It's a question we're all asked at one time or another when we know we're in a bad relationship that we can't seem to get out of.

Why *didn't* I leave? Because at that point my self-esteem was completely tied up in making Peter see that I was indeed enough – that I *didn't deserve* to be treated like that. And by that time, who I was, was a victim. That was my identity and so everything that happened just continued to support that idea of myself. With each boundary that I lifted for Peter, with each abuse I allowed, I further created for myself an identity that didn't allow for anything *but* maltreatment.

So what could I do? How could I change my situation? I had become so used to feeling angry and sorry for myself that I'd nearly forgotten all the spiritual lessons I'd learned. And then a little voice in me said, 'Start praying.' So I did, slowly and sheepishly at first, and then feverishly. I prayed for guidance, to find a way out of this groove I was caught in.

I also knew I didn't have the strength to leave Peter yet but started sneaking off to Twelve-Step meetings (The Twelve Steps is a fellowship support group for those dealing with various issues of addiction). I learned about the power of surrendering my problems to God and admitting that it was too much for me to handle.

All the reading I'd done, all the wisdom I thought I'd gained from all those theology books I'd read, proved useless to me now. I had obviously not really learned what I needed to learn. Desperation has a way of helping you to learn swiftly and thoroughly what works and what doesn't.

What *didn't* work was trying to get a man who had no clue on how to love, to love me. What *did* work was my own profound surrender to Grace.

Since I no longer had my work to give me a sense of personal power, I knew I had to do something that would shift my focus from the problem to things that made me feel good. So I did some investigating and found a home for children who had been abused and neglected that desperately needed volunteers. Hollygrove, also known as the Los Angeles Orphan's Home Society, took in kids who had been so traumatized that they couldn't make it in foster homes or with adopted families, and reestablished their trust and good behavior by way of therapy, art, and teaching healthy bonding. In the old days Hollygrove would have been called an orphanage; now it was called a treatment center. When I met these kids, and heard the horrific stories of their survival, I knew I'd found my work.

I started volunteering at Hollygrove by being what they called a special friend, a mentor. The first little girl assigned to me was named Latanya, and she had been badly beaten by her mother's boyfriend. At age eight she picked at and cut herself, a typical symptom of a child who has been the victim of incest, and sat for hours without talking to anyone. Latanya shared a 'cottage' at Hollygrove with about ten other girls and maniacally cleaned up after everyone – finding her peace by getting lost in tasks that would absorb all her attention.

It took me weeks of sitting patiently with Latanya before she even talked with me. But I understood her, and even though my life had never known the horrors she had already experienced by age eight, I somehow felt like we were there to help each other heal. Without talking about it, Latanya and I struggled with the same questions: What's so wrong with me that made this person act so hatefully? What can I do to change it? How can I get him to love me? I drew closer to this little girl, wishing that I could give her some wisdom but knowing that I was just as baffled as she was.

One day I brought Latanya over to my little apartment to watch some TV and she looked around in awe as if I lived in a mansion. She marveled at the size of my television set (19 inches) and at the fact that I had a washer/dryer in the closet. I had a bowl of candy on the coffee table and my newly adopted Chihuahua was lying in the sun near the window. All of this fascinated and delighted this child who had had to knock on neighbors' doors when she was too hungry to stand it anymore.

Suddenly, a light went on for me. I had so much to be grateful for, and somewhere along the way I had stopped seeing it. I had beauty all around me: I had food to eat, a pet to love, and an apartment to sleep in. I had my youth, my future, my Twelve Steps meetings, and, most dramatically, I had this child in front of me to show me that I was an adult who could choose rather than a child who could not. It may sound melodramatic, but in that moment something deep inside me shifted. Instead of lamenting what I didn't have, I saw all the gifts around me. Instead of feeling helpless, I was helping someone. And instead of being thoroughly depressed, I found myself blissfully happy.

In that moment gratitude changed me from the woman who felt sorry for herself, to the woman who had so much that her 'cup runneth over.' And then the answers to those questions came: there was nothing wrong with me, just as there was nothing wrong with Latanya. We had to learn that we were lovable despite the twisted messages given us. We couldn't *make* someone love us who didn't know how to love. We couldn't change them, but we could choose not to believe them.

After this moment of new clarity, I started seeing Peter with different eyes. Rather than reflecting back to me my apparent self-loathing, I saw Peter as the wounded spirit that he was. I held no grudge against him; I just knew that we needed to stop doing this dance. So each and every time I was with him, I prayed under my breath, 'Thank you, God, for helping me to leave this situation.' Or 'Thank you, God, for giving me the courage, the guidance, the words, and the strength to move on.' I figured that since gratitude had shifted my outlook so profoundly before, I was going to apply that principle of recognizing the good wherever I might need to be empowered by its great healing power.

By saying thank you all the time, I really started *feeling* as if I were someone who had a lot to be grateful for. I became that person. I regularly took Latanya on 'outings' to enjoy the simple pleasures of the dog park, or to the movies, or out to lunch at Denny's. Nothing could have been more healing to me than to see that child happy for an hour or two. I was doing something nice for her, but it was she who brought me the great gift of learning about the healing and manifesting power of gratitude. She felt good, which made me feel good about myself. And that allowed me to see how lucky I was, which brought me to back to gratitude, which magically seemed to bring about *more* to be grateful for. I had learned a great lesson in trying to make sense of Latanya's situation, and for that I was also deeply grateful.

My addiction to Peter was weakening as I grew stronger, and I kept inching farther and farther away from him. I kept thanking God for the miraculous way things would unfold. And then they did. Note here, please, that I was thankful *before* I got what I wanted. I *assumed* that the good outcome was already mine.

Since Peter was such a top-notch negotiator, I'd struggled immensely with his grilling verbal attacks on me. No matter what the charge – usually he accused me of flirting with another man, which then gave him permission to act out violently and then cheat – I could not seem to defend myself. Even though I never dared do anything that would upset him, he found a way to paint me as the dirty criminal who had wronged him and deserved punishment.

The thing about addictive relationships is that they are in no way logical or reasonable – one cannot appeal to either party by way of debate. So with my prayers of gratitude I simply said 'Thank you' for having everything magically take care of itself. And it did. On every level.

I somehow found the words to shut Peter down – I don't even remember what they were, because they didn't seem like they came from me; rather, they came *through* me. But whatever I said, or what God said through me, stopped his haranguing. And from out of that same pool of inspiration, I was able to pick myself up and finally leave him.

Oddly enough, the phone also started ringing with work opportunities. I stayed in Twelve Steps, started therapy, prayed and meditated regularly, and deepened my commitment to Hollygrove and the kids there. Every day I had more gratitude for the healing that was going on for me, and with each ensuing day more good things presented themselves to be grateful for.

Somehow through the darkest incarnation of my self-loathing, I had found the source of all the good that would ever come to me: gratitude. I'd read about it and certainly understood it intellectually, but it was only when I was brought to my knees by my own 'dark night of the soul' that I could see it, taste it, and feel it in my bones. I clung to gratitude and it delivered me.

Certainly there were days that didn't feel so rosy. I had many cold hard realities to face. I was too old to resuscitate my modeling career. I couldn't afford regular therapy. And the three and a half years with Peter left me with some haunting memories. So I would find little things to be grateful for: that I lived in sunny California, for fresh squeezed grapefruit juice in the morning, for the hikes that invigorated my spirit. And more than anything, Latanya, who showed me that if an eight-year-old little spirit could survive what she did and become childlike and playful again, so could I.

Recovering the spirit is a deeply rewarding and empowering task; I can't imagine anyone setting out to experience the 'dark night' just to learn this lesson. But I suspect our souls know, on some level, that it's a good thing, an enriching experience to come through the darkness, and it's the soul in constant contact with God that guides us toward our higher realization.

CHARITY

We sometimes resist finding our gratitude because we think it will take our attention off something we need to solve, and in a way it does. It forces us to look at what *is* working, and thus our energy stops interfering with a troublesome situation. When we move aside, Grace moves in to heal the pain.

Finding gratitude is as simple as taking a deep breath and appreciating the moment. That right here, right now, everything is exactly as it should be. And that you have come to this moment for a reason you might still be unaware of, but it is beautiful in its simple perfection. Just take a minute now, and look around you to acknowledge all the things that make you happy. Feel it, absorb it, and give thanks out loud so that not only God hears it, but you do too.

Start off small and then expand to the big things, like how you healed from a wicked flu or passed a dreaded test in class. After finding your gratitude, you will naturally want to express it in some way. The best way I know to accomplish that, as my own story demonstrates, is by doing service.

Charity in the old sense of the word alludes to one who is superior in the having of things, and giving to one who is lacking and in need. Unfortunately, this way of looking at service points to a separation in people, making one feel above and the other in a position of weakened dependence. True charity, in fact, is that which balances the energy and/or the material goods.

> To give of ourselves is to be open vessels through which miracles can flow.

To give in the spirit of 'looking good,' or because it's seen to be the right thing to do, negates the spiritual quality that charity stands for. To describe yourself as benevolent and giving because some other poor person doesn't have what you do is to not see them as your brother, equal in the eyes of God. In fact, it sets up a sort of resentment between the giver and the receiver, being that the roles become more polarized. The energy that is created by a charitable gesture depends completely on the spirit in which it is given.

For example, if you give a homeless person on the street corner twenty dollars but you give it thinking that he is incapable of being a healthy, participating person in society, you are in fact punctuating that part of him. You are underscoring exactly that part of him that he needs to overcome. The trick is to give in the spirit of nonjudgment, to see the potential in the person and aid it to come to fruition. All action rides the trail of belief and perception, so it is our intention, which is always being telepathically communicated, that we have to monitor in every act of charity. So even though we think we're doing something good by being charitable, if not done in the right spirit we can in fact be quite damaging.

The true spirit of charity is giving out of a place of evergreen abundance, knowing that no thing, no attachment, is ours to claim in the first place. Instead, we are vessels through which universal abundance flows. In the area of relationships, being charitable means giving of your love, of your attention, of your affection, and of your intimacy, without seeing yourself as better than your partner.

> *It is possible to give without loving, but it is impossible to love without giving.*
> —RICHARD BRAUNSTEIN

Perhaps in the process of reading this book, or through other life-affirming experiences, you have become more fully aware of the good that already exists in the world. Charity, then, would be the freely given reciprocation of that – that, because of who you have become, another might be affected and lifted by your energy.

Charity begins not only at home but also in our hearts and our minds, and our very perceptions. The task at hand is not only to be giving of ourselves, but also to literally *see* people through the perception that we are indeed equal and perfect in God's eyes, and deserving of the same honor, respect, and kindness. If everyone were to adopt that nature, there would be no need for funds set up or organizations to rescue, because the natural order would be to take care of each other moment by moment. To see someone in need would not stir the reaction of pity inside us, but instead the reaction of, 'oh, this is what they need, lucky me, I have that to supply,' and it would be done.

Mantra

I am a naturally generous person.

When you yourself are full of the spirit of abundance, it is only natural that you would want to give the source of the very same away. By doing service both the giver and the receiver get to feel good. Both are equals, both are benefiting from the flow of energy.

By being charitable and doing service, you create the space inside you to receive great love in a way previously not experienced. Being a person without judgment creates an opening for others to be able to see that very perfection in you. Another perk of doing service is that even if the charitable act has nothing to do with the area of relationships, a reciprocal energy is activated by the *giving*. So you don't know how your good work is going to come back to you. All that you need to be aware of is that you are creating good karma.

> *Each moment of our lives, each moment that is given to us to live, we have to live very deeply. If you are capable of living deeply one moment of your life, you can learn to live the same way all the other moments of your life. ... Each moment is a chance for us to make peace with the world, to make peace possible for the world, to make happiness possible for the world. The world needs our happiness.*
>
> —THICH NHAT HANH, *Teachings on Love*

DISCREDITING THE MYTHS

In my own experience of finding gratitude, I came up against certain blocks that I found were quite common with my friends and clients as well. We cling to certain beliefs, thinking that to be truly grateful would mean giving up a big piece of our power. This again is the ego at work trying to preserve its position of control, rather than guidance from our true spiritual nature. There are so many myths about gratitude. Let's take a look at some of them and see which ones you may be unconsciously living by.

MYTHS ABOUT GRATITUDE

Myth: If I am grateful for my present situation, I am saying that I'm satisfied with what I have and then cannot hope for something more.

Reality: When we are grateful, the Trinity Self experiences abundance, thereby programming our nature for even more of the same. Once we can experience in the core of our being that feeling of being full and even overflowing, it becomes natural to gravitate toward more situations that will confirm, again, that internally held belief that we are being taken care of.

Myth: If I am grateful, I will stop caring for and about myself.

Reality: Being grateful means seeing the perfection in every situation and person. If we feel thankful we don't have to be self-obsessed, always trying to fill the hole. When we're narcissistic like that, we can't see past our own neurosis, which sets up a block for anything new to come in. The irony is that the more service we do because of our gratitude, the more we become compassionate with ourselves as well as becoming more dynamically connected to every human being. Not only is everyone served by our being grateful, but the Self is ultimately the winner as well.

Myth: Gratitude makes me a sucker. It makes me happy to have a booby prize.

Reality: In fact, having gratitude doesn't just humble us and force us to be happy with what we're stuck with, but indicates that we are appreciative of all the good we already have. Being appreciative makes people want to do more for us, so in the end we do get the big prize after all.

Myth: If I get too grateful, I won't be motivated or ambitious to move forward.

Reality: Gratitude doesn't make us lazy; it inspires us to get more of that feeling. The bliss that we feel by recognizing the miracles that are already in our lives energizes and inspires us to perpetuate that very energy.

Myth: If I am grateful, I'll feel small and diminished by a 'meek' stance in a tough world.

Reality: Being thankful comes from a position of confidence and not weakness at all. It is the strong person who knows that the interplay of reality is giving and receiving, yin and yang, upward pushing motion and downward receiving motion. Gratitude is a show of strength, which fortifies not only the giver but the receiver as well. Being modest is a virtue because humility makes us approachable. On the other hand, the arrogance of not recognizing when we have been given a gift turns away the energy of confirming good.

See how easy it is to slip back into fear-based thinking? We need to constantly remind ourselves of the simple laws of karma and reciprocation. Nothing makes more sense than to see the simplicity laid before us; we acknowledge the good by giving love, and by giving love we attract more good things to us.

EXERCISE: GRATITUDE MANIFESTATION

Let's try an exercise here to illustrate how gratitude manifests more of the same.

1. Think of something you are really grateful for. Write it down here.

     _____

2. Meditate on what it feels like to appreciate this particular thing or person.

     _____

3. If you follow the feeling, what does it make you want to do?

     _____

4. Assuming you do that action, what happens next?

_____

By creating a loving experience for someone, you yourself also experience the gesture. The fact of giving naturally draws to you the reciprocal energy. Notice how you started with acknowledging what was good and how it then became a springboard for you to keep that energy circulating.

When you really *get* how lucky you are, how really blessed, it becomes almost *necessary* to express that gratitude by moving the energy forward to benefit someone else. Obligation plays no part in this; this step is about the natural flow of giving and receiving, acknowledging and presenting.

MEDITATION ON GRATITUDE

Let's integrate this step into your cellular programming.

Retreat to your sanctuary, lie down, and close your eyes. Breathing deeply, get very comfortable in your body in this room at this particular point in time. Relax all your muscles, let go of any tension, and become very present.

As you breathe in, feel the health of your body supporting this effort; your lungs that are working for you, the muscles that enable you to be strong, your heart which is open and loving, and your mind which has grasped a new level of thinking and perception.

Feel in your very bones the satisfaction of this moment;

the quietness, the focus, the journey that you are under-taking. And breathe into this endeavor.

Now call to mind the things that bring you joy. They can be small, like having waffles for breakfast; or large, like being given a raise at work. With each thing you are appreciating call to mind the energy behind them, the force of love that has gifted you with this experience. Breathe into it.

Now let this feeling of gratitude intensify, let it lift you to your highest vibration, your highest potential of Self. And with your entire Trinity Self give thanks to God for all of this love that has been present in your life. And, know-ing what is on the way, give thanks in advance for the abundance of love.

Knowing that your soul mate is on the horizon, thank God for all the experience that has brought you to this point. Notice how your goal of finding the relationship has been a great motivator for spiritual growth, and thank the universal mind for helping to unfold things, gently, easily, and perfectly.

This gratitude fuels the transformation and you will be amazed at how this shift in your attitude draws to you even greater good.

Take a deep breath now and let resonate within you the gratitude and glory for the partnership that is about to unfold. When you get to the point of feeling as if you are full and overflowing, let it click into place, and settle into your energy. Then gently open your eyes and go back into your day.

THE CONNECTING FACTOR

When you have gratitude, you no longer take things for granted. You acknowledge the sacredness of the small things in life, as well as the grand. Each moment becomes a gift, a reflection of the intentions you've chosen to live by.

To find and express your gratitude gives you a profound empathy through which you get in touch with other human beings at their most honorable level. This enables you to transcend any narcissistic boundaries and open yourself to the possibility of Grace and its miracles. Strategically speaking, gratitude takes the attention off of yourself. When the attention is off, you're free to receive something greater than what your own small-minded self could possibly manufacture.

Mantra

I am grateful for the knowledge that my partner is approaching.

Say you meet someone who has a lot of the qualities you are looking for. Rather than noticing what's missing, you are now ready to put your attention on what you appreciate. By doing so you connect with those qualities you love, which will naturally bring forth more of that essence. This could come in the form of the person in front of you turning out to be more of what you were looking for than you'd originally thought. Or, since you are now resonating with those qualities, someone else would soon approach embodying those characteristics with even *more* of what would make you happy.

To expect more without being grateful for what has already shown up doesn't make sense. You're telling the universal mind that the abundance you already *do* have doesn't impress you.

If you want to find love, you need to notice and connect with that love. Anything you'd like to receive, you must first give of freely. Being grateful serves as a reminder, as a force of love and abundance that is always at work. Even if something at the time doesn't seem 'right,' appreciate it and assume it's bringing you some sort of gift that in the end you will indeed be grateful for. And instead of waiting till it shows up the way you want it, give thanks for it now, to hasten the manifesting.

By our compassion we are connected to the higher nature of all human beings, and gravitate to those who share our path.

To tap into the universal flow, we need to practice gratitude on a regular and unswerving basis. Consistently acknowledge that which is good in your life and give a hardy thanks by doing service for others. Give of yourself that which you wish to receive. Find the sacred gift in each moment and bless it by your recognition of it as a miracle. Because gratitude is indeed the maker of miracles.

Seven Everyday Tips to Assist in Step 6, Finding and Expressing Gratitude:

1. Do some volunteer work so you get to bask in the residual good feeling.

2. Take basic good care of yourself: eat well, rest, play, etc. Consciously feel how blessed you are to be able to do these simple things.

3. Bless in someone else those qualities you wish to manifest for yourself.

4. Say Grace before every meal to ritualize your gratitude.

5. Begin saying 'Thank you,' even if just under your breath, for every little kindness the world shows.

6. When an unpleasant situation arises, thank the players for giving you the opportunity to rise to your best self in the face of adversity.

7. Every time you wish for something *more* to happen in your life, find something you didn't stop and appreciate and punctuate it with gratitude.

Stay the Course

There is a vitality, a life force, a quickening that is translated through you into action. . . . It is not your business to determine how good it is, nor how it compares with other expression. It is your business to keep it yours clearly and directly, to keep the channel open. You do not even have to believe in yourself or your work. You have to keep open and aware directly to the urges that motivate you. Keep the channel open.

—MARTHA GRAHAM

At this point you can rest assured, knowing that with the footwork done now you only need to keep the process moving forward. By being still and opening to an inner truth, you have awakened the spirit of transformation. You have done the exercises, committed to the rituals of your spiritual practice, and have been thankful. It's as if you were in class and have graduated, and now are ready to go out into the world to apply the skills you've learned.

Challenges will inevitably arise and you will, from time to time, wonder at your footing. You may take two steps forward and one step back, but overall the movement will have a progressive quality.

How your miracle arrives and unfolds is, and will always be, a divine mystery. You could never know the series of events that must take place to frame perfectly the meeting of your partner. It is not your business to dictate to the universe how you think things should show up: Your business is to stay the course. Even if you 'get' the lessons, they need to settle in and become integrated.

The organic process of becoming and attracting a great partner needs constant nourishment. In a way it's as if you've gone through sort of a spiritual rehab, detoxed, and found your sacred power. And you have to take it one day at a time, being grateful for each moment that you're able to connect in a meaningful way with yourself and those around you.

When people come out of rehab they are given a program of 'aftercare' to follow. You might think of this final step of my miracles course as your very own, personalized aftercare program, so that you might continue growing in spirit and in magnetism.

TRUST DIVINE TIMING

When we try to impress upon the world our sense of what's right and how things should show up, we are sending a message that we don't trust in a divine unfolding of our path. To try and rush things would be to steal from the absolute perfection that is in store for us. It is vital that you understand that everything has its time; everything has its place.

> *To every thing there is a season, a time for every purpose under the sun . . .*
> —ECCLESIASTES 3:1-8

Think of all the times you have only recognized critical turning points in your life in hindsight; how, even though things might have been painful or seemed to have taken forever, afterward you were able to see that there were powerful reasons for why they happened the way they did. Consider also that your future partner may now be unraveling him or herself from whatever entanglement they're in. Your partner could very well be on his or her way, but details unbeknownst to you must be tended to.

And consider your own soul's timing, it's own readiness in being in a relationship. You are ever-evolving and your soul knows when that evolution should include a partner. You might have more growing or self-searching to do before making a union. In the scheme of development, certain things have to take place, such as your *ability to accept* something great, so it doesn't shock the system and therefore get rejected. We can't force readiness, it is something that happens organically without our coercion: we can take the steps to put the process in motion, but we can not dictate the exact sequencing of unfoldment.

Mantra

My partner comes at the perfect time and in the perfect way.

Assume that the time will occur naturally when all elements are at their ready and come together with synchronicity. What might seem like serendipity will be God's wink to the preparation you've done. Think of how much you've changed even in the past month just by the daily experiences you deal with; and then think about how different you are from one year ago, five years ago, ten years ago. Trust the quiet unfolding of your spiritual maturity to attract that very readiness in your mate. Be patient; let the fruit ripen, let the seeds grow into flowers, let nature take its course.

KEEP IT TO YOURSELF

Sometimes, out of a desire for camaraderie, we can find ourselves discussing our relationship problems with our friends. It's a perfectly natural desire – to want to know ourselves better by bouncing our experiences off other people. But you are not like everybody else, and since you've just done all this work on yourself, I would suggest that you keep it to yourself for a while. The last thing you need right now is to see the squint of cynicism or the glance of pity from someone who thinks that you're being a dreamer.

Even though they don't mean to, the people closest to you can cast doubt on your process of transformation because they haven't done the work to know where your confidence is rooted. Understand that it is not malicious intent but rather their own fear and need for control that keeps them from believing the great potential of the miraculous. Why expose yourself to their old assumptions and beliefs?

No, the precious idea you are trying to manifest needs the safety and privacy of the intense growth process that is taking place within you. To be introduced to the outside world too soon would expose the creation to negative and confusing energy, a vulnerable environment, and dissipating influences. For this reason it's important to keep your development private. You and only you will know when it is time to introduce to the world this new way of being.

> In the privacy of spiritual communion, all things reveal themselves by way of intimate unfolding.

∞

Chloe was a marketing professional in a very prestigious firm. She prided herself on her ingenuity and her ability to get what she wanted from people. It's what made her successful in her field. However, Chloe hadn't been able to find a man who she really clicked with. Her dating history had been filled with all kinds of different experiences, the only common link being a general feeling of dissatisfaction and frustration. Chloe was smart enough, and open enough, to know that the answer had to lie within, and that was where she needed to start if she was ever going to find herself in a relationship that was fulfilling and lasting.

Being the kind of person who is thorough as well as creative, Chloe took on the process of transformation wholeheartedly, going through each of the steps as I presented them to her with enthusiasm and a wonderful sense of discovery. I could tell that she'd be a changed woman by the time she was done just by the way her energy radiated wonder and acceptance. Chloe was especially affected by the meditations (the same ones you are learning here) and practiced them every day for twenty minutes at a time. She referred to those times as her 'sacred breath.' And after looking deeply within and magnetizing what she knew to be the right kind of partnership for her, Chloe was able to detach from the focus she'd created and let events unfold naturally.

But a couple of unforeseen problems arose: problems that resulted from stepping beyond the bounds of who she was before she started the process. Going through what felt like a rebirthing of her soul through the same step-by-step process you've been learning here was exhilarating to Chloe; enough so, in fact, that she couldn't help but tell practically everyone she knew about her experience. She was so sure she was going to meet the right man that she told everyone exactly what he'd be like. It was the one breakdown in her 'very together' demeanor. Chloe went over her ideal mate's profession, the way he looked, the way he handled a relationship, everything. She told her friends all this not out of hopeful obsession, but more from a sense of sureness about what she really wanted, which she'd never defined before. It was that sureness that was joyful to her, and she wanted to share it.

But the reactions from her friends did not match Chloe's own enthusiasm. They thought she was being naïve and overly trusting from something she had no control over. Fate, they said, could never be so rich as her dream life. They kept reminding Chloe of her past, of all the disappointments, and made sure she knew that, given who she was she shouldn't expect that men were any other way than who they'd always been. And what was worse was that they communicated this to Chloe by way of concerned conversation, letting her know that they really cared for her and didn't want to see her get hurt.

What her friends unconsciously didn't want, though, was for Chloe to be happy, because then she'd no longer be the Chloe who always needed comforting and advice. She wouldn't be the same person they became friends with, and they'd have to adjust their roles in order to remain friends. Chloe was a very powerful woman in many ways, and I think that her friends felt that the one thing they had over her – and remember, this is unconscious – was her inability to master relationships. So they felt threatened and began to deflate Chloe's hope, enthusiasm, and faith in Grace. These being her very good friends, she listened.

Chloe began to doubt herself and what she'd achieved. It was hard for her to maintain her energy and sureness in the face of reasonable doubt. She began to go right back to the old patterns that had held her in check in the past, and her friends embraced her unhappiness like a lost relative returned. The man she'd been waiting for, who she'd worked on herself to make room for and magnetize, never did appear. At least she had friends who loved her, she thought.

During a guided meditation designed to get clarity I asked Chloe what was holding her back. She responded instinctively that she didn't want to lose her friends and she would if she stayed her course of transformation. What Chloe finally came to realize was that her friends were certainly not malicious in intent, but they were having a negative effect on her ability to move forward. This is when it became clear that there was no alternative but to cull them from her life, lovingly and clearly. There could be no ambiguity because, in that gray space, all the old stuff would have a place to flourish again.

I am happy to report that Chloe found her way. She doesn't have the same circle of friends as before, but she has new ones who feel comfortable with her confidence and exuberance. They became her friends when she was strong, full of faith, and magnetic, and they remain friends who want to see the best for her to this day. And, of course, the best thing is that Chloe did, finally, meet the man.

Don't be surprised if some people drop out of your life. Your friends may not like it when you change because your light will expose the darkness they may still be attached to. When you make changes on the inside, it is only natural that changes will take place in every area of your life. I would urge you to just roll with it; things will find their balance, and harmony will soon be in place.

MAKE CHOICES THAT SUPPORT YOU

Everything you do from here on out will be a reflection of your choice to come from love rather than fear. This will reverberate in every area of your life: what you choose to work on, who you choose to have in your life, and how you perceive the world around you.

Remember that being passive lets your energy fall into maladaptive grooves. The mission here is to construct a world around you that supports the new, authentic interior life you've created. Find people whose energy lifts you and who share the vision of possibility and enlightenment.

The work that you do is also a reflection of your commitment to your higher nature: because that which you invest your energy in is what will be reflected back to you. Have no doubt you will be presented with choices, and tempting ones at that. Every choice you make, though, is a testament to what you believe.

More than declaring something or theorizing about any truth, it is your actions that tell the universal mind who you are and what should come your way. You may find that you make small changes such as, 'I'm not going to the gym anymore,' but instead, 'I'm going to hike so I can be in nature,' or perhaps you may take a break from being around family and old messages you need not hear for awhile. You may choose to talk on the phone less and keep a journal more regularly. Whatever it is, be conscious of the soul's impulses to grow and direct you to love and make your choices according to the love that guides you.

In the next several sections, we'll talk about how to handle meeting new people. We want to now be able to bring together what has been developing on the inside with what shows up on the outside.

MAINTAIN HEALTHY BOUNDARIES

When you meet someone you're interested in, I recommend that you get to know who they are slowly. Impose no projections on them and require that they do the same for you. I don't mean you need to verbally state your boundaries, per se, but knowing and understanding where you are comfortable will be telepathically communicated to the person before you. Again, maintain a certain amount of privacy (which in fact will come across as mystery and is always alluring!) and respect their vulnerabilities as well.

Mantra

I am lovingly protected by the instincts of my Higher Mind.

You cannot anticipate someone else's needs, nor can you expect them to anticipate yours. Try to maintain an inter-dependence with whomever comes your way: independent and self-sufficient but engaging in healthy relatedness. Keep your own schedule, resisting the temptation to throw yourself wholly into someone else's life. Although it might feel good at first, if you let yourself become engulfed, you'll eventually feel as if you lost something precious. Keep aware of your personal priorities and make sure that the new relationship (or quest for one) doesn't overwhelm you and supplant your own concerns.

Invite your new partner unhurriedly into your world and your circle of friends. Don't thrust upon him or her an entirely new cast of characters to get to know. Gently integrate your lives.

Make sure you maintain your own personal values, morals, and spiritual codes. Keep your self-respect in high regard; it has been hard-earned by all this internal self-searching. One way to lose your self-respect is by sacrificing your finer beliefs in an effort to morph into someone's projection of you just because you think you've found the Right One. Don't give up your sense of selfhood; if s/he is in fact the Right One, s/he won't want you to anyway.

And, remember, just because you have grown doesn't mean you won't be presented with old situations that still pull your strings. Should an experience present itself that hints of the old unhealthy energy, firmly say 'no' and walk away.

BOUNDARY EXERCISE

Make a list of three loving boundaries. Write why they are important, and how they have been erected from love rather than fear. Then write how you are going to maintain them.

For example:

Boundary to Keep: I will not have sex until I feel safe and in love.

Why It's Important: Because I know I'm vulnerable to low self-esteem if I give myself away sexually without being in love.

How to Keep It: By being clear and vocal about what I'm comfortable with.

Boundary to Keep: 1. _____
                       2. _____
                       3. _____

Why It's Important: 1. _____
                         2. _____
                         3. _____

How to Keep It: 1. _____
                     2. _____
                     3. _____

It's crucial to have boundaries but not to get caught up in the rigidity of them. The idea is to float them but not to be oppressed by them. Honor yourself by lovingly maintaining boundaries.

CREATE AN ENVIRONMENT THAT'S CONDUCIVE TO LOVE

If you could imagine what you want your world to look like, then you have the ability to begin creating it now. The soul revels in beauty, in balance, harmony, and in an inspiring setting. So by creating a place that is conducive to energetic alchemy, you are acknowledging and cooperating with the fact that we are constantly influenced by our environment.

You can use the time that you are still alone to make your home a productive sanctuary for healing and manifesting. Write down your mantras and tape them to the bathroom mirror or refrigerator. Have beautiful music playing that lifts your spirit and your mood. Prepare delicious meals to celebrate the company of your newfound self. If you don't have one, consider adopting a pet so that the feeling of unconditional love and companionship is tangible.

This time of waiting is limited and temporary so find the rewards of having your own personal space. Infuse it with love and poetry and cheerfulness. Make sure that you carve out a space that is designated for prayer and meditation so that you might always have a place to go for clarity and inspiration. Another thing I like to do is to ritualize the feeling of transformation by burning candles with prayers written on them, or clearing the energy of my home with sage and sweet grass. Take the time to enjoy your space, make it your church, your laboratory for miracles.

BE SURE NOT TO CONFUSE FANTASY WITH REALITY

I know we've been talking about using the imagination to conjure up the image of your soul mate, but let's be careful to note that fantasy belongs just where it develops: in the mind.

A fantasy is used to generate the energy that, in turn, gives us direction, intention, passion, and hope. But it is not something to be clung to or measured against. Anything that is real will have rough spots and gray areas, and not conform exactly to our vision. We have to honor the whole of any situation rather than pick it apart and reject that which does not fit with our fantasy ideals.

The finely honed mental picture is the guiding map which delivers us to a new level, to something that vaults us out of what was old and familiar. But if we hold too tightly to it, we are in fact denying ourselves the rich experience of chance and of being surprised.

Sometimes people might be more comfortable in fantasy rather than venturing out into the real world. But that is an escape and a way of avoiding growth. We don't have to take risks if we live entirely in our own little world; real life calls for us to go out on a limb and take chances that might seem frightening or unfamiliar.

[For the Buddhist] the external world and his inner world are for him only two sides of the same fabric, in which the threads of all forces and of all events, of all forms of consciousness and of their objects are woven into an inseparable net of endless, mutually conditioned relations.

—LAMA ANAGARIKA GOVINDA

We can weave together our dreams, our fantasies, with our everyday life. But to expect one to conform to the other sets us up for disappointment. Keep dreaming, and keep meditating on your sensory image. But also let it recede throughout the day to your peripheral vision, so that you might keep your heart inspired by the mystical and unknown while your instincts remain grounded in reality.

Another important thing to keep in mind here is to stay realistic. We don't always get everything we want, but if we go with the flow we do usually get better than what we could hope for.

Nothing is perfect. And yet everything is perfect just the way it is.

HOW WILL YOU KNOW WHEN YOU MEET THE RIGHT ONE?

Even though you are now living in the condition of expecting the miracle, you don't want to be tapping your fingers and wondering if every person you meet might be The One. That takes away the magic, for one thing; for another, it hinders your possibilities because it involves the ego. But if you suspect that perhaps the person in front of you is *it*, close your eyes and ask yourself. You'll know, you'll hear the answer. The feeling will be a natural but exciting one. It will feel like a quiet recognition of what you always knew would happen.

The very best gauge of whether or not you've met the partner you seek is to see who you become in their presence. Do you like yourself? Do you have interesting things to talk about? Do you bring out the best in each other? Is your creative energy at full tilt?

Sometimes you do hear bells and whistles, and sometimes you can look across the room and get that feeling in your gut that you're beholding your life's partner. However it's just as likely that the recognition of your soul mate will be slow and gradual. You will meet a really wonderful person and find that you want to know more about him/her with each passing day. That's how you'll know.

When the soul is ready the mate appears.

Meeting your soul mate is certainly exhilarating. You feel completely alive and connected and comfortable with yourself. Still another factor you want to consider is whether or not you are being guided by your Higher Power. When you enter into a spiritual relationship with someone every aspect of your Trinity Self should be alighted by their presence, and by that harmony should appear the Mystical Third, Grace. Ask yourself: Does this relationship include the luminous presence of the Mystical Third?

When you do meet The One you will respond to them in ways you didn't know you had within. Your personality will become richer, your body will feel stronger, and your spirit will seem like it's flying high. There is no test to take that will prove that the one standing in front of you is meant to be your mate. But again, get quiet and listen to your inner guidance: the answer will become apparent. And until it does, just enjoy getting to know this new soul. Rather than judging the potential right away or projecting your fantasy onto this person, just quietly be in his/her presence with openness and the intention to see the truth. And with the courage to take a risk, take the leap!

DETACH FROM THE DETAILS

As they say in Twelve-Step programs, 'The details are not your business!' What *is* your business is to keep yourself as clear and full of integrity as possible from moment to moment.

If you've done the work and the sensory image is at the periphery of your consciousness, the miracle of finding a great relationship is well on its way. But remember this: Anything you could possibly want for yourself is far less than God intends for you; so being stuck on particulars compromises your potential. For instance, if you imagine someone with blond hair, blue eyes, who loves to sail, and you meet someone who has brown hair, green eyes, and hates sailing, don't write him off because he doesn't fit the picture exactly. What's far more important is the person's essence, the feeling response you have to him, and how his energy affects you.

So many things about us are susceptible to change: the way we dress, our hobbies, even our goals in life, so to limit yourself because someone doesn't look exactly how you think he or she should look is really to be stuck in the small picture. Would you like it if someone rejected you because you didn't have just the right style? Or the ideal job? Those things change all the time and shouldn't be deciding factors.

Let me be very clear, though, that I'm not saying that you can change someone, nor should you try. Only that you never know what someone's path has in store for them. What's far more important is how you feel in this person's presence, the quality of your connection.

Remember also that accepting the person in front of you opens the door for them to become their full potential. Don't worry about whether someone is successful enough or creative enough; the integrity of your energy will lock in with its perfect match. You will not have to force anything, nor will you need to concede that which is really comfortable. That's a great gift to give, seeing someone's possibilities, so let go of any preconceived ideas of how things should look and just keep choosing to perceive with love.

The best you can do is control your intention and your energy and let God take care of the details.

> *Non-action does not mean doing nothing and keeping silent. Let everything be allowed to do what it naturally does, so that its nature will be satisfied.*
> —FROM THE CHAUNG-TZU

EXERCISE: GAUGE YOUR MICROMANAGING FACTOR

Some of us are so used to handling every little detail that we don't even know how to detach. It takes a conscious effort to let go and not bog down our energy with constant micromanaging. There is a time to be 'controlling,' such as being disciplinary with kids or organizing your work schedule. But if you think you have to have every single detail under your watchful eye, you are staying way too attached to let anything really magical happen. So take a moment to answer 'Yes' or 'No' to the following questions.

If you answer 'Yes' to more than two, there's a good chance that you haven't really surrendered.

1. Do you go out looking to meet someone, choosing the place for the sole purpose of bumping into your soul mate?

   Yes ___ No ___

2. Do you manipulate dates by playing by 'The Rules'?

   Yes ___ No ___

3. When someone says they'll call, do you tap your fingers whilst waiting to see if they follow through?

   Yes ___ No ___

4. Are you trying to change someone you're seeing into someone you think they *can be*?

   Yes ___ No ___

5. Are you brushing off answers that you don't like when getting to know someone?

   Yes ___ No ___

6. Are you telling your dates what they're capable of in their lives and coaching them on what they *should* be doing?

   Yes ___ No ___

7. Are you angry with someone you're dating because things aren't going exactly the way you want them to?

   Yes ___ No ___

8. Are you opening doors and closets to find out all of this person's secrets?

   Yes ___ No ___

9. Do you police this person's actions and whereabouts?
   Yes ___ No ___

10. Are you *using* spiritual practice in a way to maneuver
    things to be exactly the way you want them?
    Yes ___ No ___

11. Do you feel like you have to be involved in most every
    aspect at work as well as home, fearing that if you aren't
    things will indeed fall apart?
    Yes ___ No ___

Don't say no too quickly. Take an honest look at yourself
and just continue to surrender where you remain attached.
And if you find yourself thinking that things would just fall
to pieces if you really let go, remember that that's precisely
what you have to risk to prove to yourself that you have
faith in the Higher Power that is always looking out for
you.

MAINTAIN YOUR ENERGY

You have a lot to be excited about. Certainly meeting your
soul mate is something to look forward to, but it's important to control your enthusiasm so that you remain
balanced and grounded in your life. Nobody needs to hear
every detail of your process, progress, and how you realize
all these deep understandings of yourself and the workings

of your life; they have their own paths to travel. Simply enjoy your enthusiasm but don't let it wear you out. A harmonious person balances their energy.

Don't misunderstand. Enthusiasm is wonderful. Indeed, such energy generates more of the same. But don't go so far as to set yourself up for disappointment if life is not able to meet your heightened expectations at every moment. You don't want to overdo it because the subconscious seeks to balance itself out. Just like the way a child who plays himself out can crash, so we must gently ride the wave of our good feeling.

> It is by way of joyful balance that the soul is lifted and celebrated.

On the other side of any great emotion lies its opposite; so to go into a hyper state of excitement naturally calls for an equal dip in mood at some point. That's not a bad thing but needs to be taken into consideration.

TEND YOUR GARDEN

Our lives are like gardens that we need to tend to through the seasons and over the years. We plant seeds as our dreams, we till them with our intentions and we harvest them by our gratitude. It is not only our right to enjoy this little piece of the universe that was given us, but it's our responsibility to take care of it.

So in matters of your garden, be sure that you are paying attention and giving energy to that which you are responsible for. Tend to your creativity, your work life, and your children if you have them. Take care of the world you come in contact with. Be responsible for how you affect your little corner of the universe. By this I mean not just obsessing on relationship life, but doing the things you need to do in a well-rounded way. Out of this fertile ground the great miracle of a spiritual relationship can be pollinated and grown.

We must cultivate our own garden.

—Voltaire

Keep Moving Forward

I love it when people say that when one door closes, another opens. What they never mention is the hallway in between. The hallway can sometimes seem to stretch on for miles, but you've just got to stay confident in the Grace that is guiding you, and that you may find your way through the next door.

Indeed when one relationship ends, the next is just around the corner, waiting. But sometimes you have to venture through the dark unknown until divine will intercedes to show the way. Patience, patience, patience. Take in the paintings on the wall, the windows that you pass, the textures around you, as you move toward the doorway of perfect partnership. The journey's end might turn out to be the journey after all, so just keep moving forward.

∞

Jim came to me because he was at a fork in the road with his marriage. He wanted clarity and direction on which way to go. We did some guided imagery and after a while, Jim realized his marriage to Sophia had gone as far as it could. He wanted children while she didn't. He wanted to be on the East Coast, she wanted to be on the West. And the whole feeling of their days was different from each other: she liked to party while he wanted a quieter life.

Jim very much believed in the sacrament of marriage and it pained him greatly to come to the conclusion that it was over. They separated, got divorced; he moved away and thinking that the next door would fling open to him, Jim became disenchanted when the love he sought did not immediately appear. Although he knew in his heart that the miracle was on its way, he could not understand why he was stuck in this seeming limbo. He lamented that he was wasting time and that perhaps he'd made a mistake. But just because he closed the door to the past did not mean that his future mate was ready to present herself at that exact moment.

We talked about using this time to cultivate his own personal garden, to create the life that he loved, whether alone or not.

When Nancy sat next to him a little over a year later in the movies, Jim wasn't even thinking of looking for a relationship (sometimes you run right into the door without seeing any signs for it). Nancy was a yoga teacher in New York who very much wanted a family, and adored Jim's contemplative nature. The magic that ignited between them was fueled by deep conversations and a willingness to take risks of all kinds. When Jim relaxed in his agenda, Nancy appeared. Had Jim not had faith that the next door would open, he would have made the mistake of forcing his way through doors that he had no business going through.

EMBRACE FAITH

Inevitably there will be periods when you have doubt and can't see what the end result is going to be. It might seem like it's taking forever to meet your soul mate, or that there appear to be no great prospects in sight. These are the times that you most need to embrace faith.

> *We must walk consciously only part way toward our goal, and then leap in the dark to our success.*
> —HENRY DAVID THOREAU

Faith, being an inner knowing, is an intuitive approach to life that is not necessarily backed up by any tangible proof. Because faith is based on the unseen world, we might not comprehend in the way that we learned throughout our lives to understand what was real, but it is our communion with God through prayer and meditation that consistently speaks to us through intuitions, hunches, and gut instinct.

Because spiritual truth overrides all physical laws, faith is often something we need to struggle with and strive for. But once things begin to show up in our lives as a result of faith, we can begin to let go, knowing our good is being looked after.

If you are in fact in a relationship already, and you're not sure where it's going to go, rather than look for a definitive answer, assume that you are in the right place at the right time, learning what you need to understand. If it's right it will become clear, as will the reverse. So if you are struggling with staying the course, take a deep breath and ask your Higher Power to fortify your faith. There will be a click of knowingness in you, an internal shift, and you will just *know* that you are going to be okay.

Guidance Prayer

God, I come to You in all of my confusion, with all of my human frailty, and I ask that You give to me the gift of faith. I see where I am unable to trust right now. I know that my smaller mind has taken control

and I cannot see the big picture. I surrender this to
You, God, and ask that whatever fear left in me be
replaced by Your mighty love. That I be guided and
directed to my perfect partner through Your divine
workings, seen and unseen. God, I ask that Your will
be done, and that the way be made clear to me. That
I might swiftly and gently be on the journey that You
have chosen for me. I thank You in advance, for I
know it is already so.
Amen

HONOR THE PATH

Assume for a moment that we are on a sacred journey, and
that each and every event that happens takes us deeper into
the truth of our soul. Every hardship, every challenge,
every emotionally packed circumstance is a lesson that we,
on some level, have agreed to learn. Rather than railing
against where we are and complaining about what we have
or don't have, we might benefit from looking at our path as
the gift that God intended it to be.

Mantra

With reverence for the sacred journey, I find my
way easily and joyfully.

If your past relationships have been painful, rather than dismissing them in your mind as mistakes, look at them as precious gems that needed to be discovered and extracted from the dense rock surrounding them. We learn from our failures; we define who we are by seeing *who we are not*. We are indeed on the sacred path of finding our soul mate; and to be irreverent about what we find along the way is to do great disservice to the Creator who guides us. Continue to be honest with yourself, to have integrity, and to greet each day with a joyful expectation of a sacred miracle unfolding. This is your path to find enlightenment, so honor those who assist you on the way and the experiences they bring you.

REMEMBER TO HAVE FUN

You have worked very hard in these seven steps, and taken a good honest look at yourself. You have gut-wrenchingly dealt with your demons and set your mind to discipline. You've committed to meditation and the contemplation of spirit and have found your humility through gratitude. Indeed, with all this in tow, you deserve to relax and have some fun! As with anything, energy needs its opposite to restore and balance itself. The serious nature of spiritual growth needs to be met with an equal amount of levity. So do something completely frivolous. Treat yourself to a manic night of dancing, or a run on the beach at night with your dogs, go out with friends and laugh till your sides ache: this is the great joy of the spirit at play.

Sometimes things may not seem to have any humor in them whatsoever, but if you stop taking things so seriously and realize that it's all just a game anyway, you can always find a little place to inject humor. Not only does a good laugh benefit your health and lighten up any situation, but it is also completely magnetic as your potential partner will be drawn to someone who thoroughly enjoys their life. Have fun, give yourself permission to go wild and shake out the stiffness that keeps the spirit from soaring.

MEDITATION: RELEASING YOUR BIRD TO FLIGHT

Go to your sanctuary and sit with your legs crossed and your eyes closed. This meditation is about sending the energy of all that you've worked on out into the universe that it might begin to take form and reflect back to you. Think of it as releasing a bird to flight; you have nurtured your soul and the request for its partner. Now it is ready to go out into the world to actualize and return to you manifest.

So take a deep breath and relax your entire body. Feel the energetic building of magnetism that is almost oozing out of you. Feel how you are in every sense ready to go on to the next stage of your life, while still completely inhabiting this precious moment. Let gather a force of momentum from the work you've done. Feel it building in strength and force. See it flowing through you and from you. And imagine yourself on the brink of the miracle of finding your perfect relationship. Breathe.

With all this building of energetic imaging, now it's time to release it. Things rarely come in exactly the way we would expect, so let go of any preconceived ideas of how the transformation should unfold. Your relationship will manifest in a far more perfect way if you surrender it to your Higher Power and trust that you are being taken care of.

Take a deep breath now, and bring that glorious golden light of Grace into your solar plexus. Let your meditation drop into that place, gather strength, and then release it into the universe. And know that is done. Feel the joy in its release.

Relax now; your work is finished. You have aligned yourself with your own highest self and programmed your subconscious for success. Keep your energy pure and the universe will work in unison to bring forth all sorts of occurrences, which could never have been foreseen. Allow the miracle to unfold. Live from an absolute certainty that you are loved and that your Great Love is indeed on the way. And so it is.

With your eyes closed and your mind open, take a deep breath and come back into the room. Smile and let it soak in.

EMBRACE THE MYSTERY

> *Beyond the beauty of the external forms, there is more*
> *here: something that cannot be named, something*
> *ineffable, some deep, inner essence. Whenever and*
> *wherever there is beauty, this inner essence shines*
> *through somehow. It only reveals itself to you when*
> *you are present. Could it be that this nameless essence*
> *and your presence are one and the same? Would it be*
> *there without your presence? Go deeply into it. Find*
> *out for yourself.*
>
> —ECKHART TOLLE, *The Power of Now*

Wouldn't life be boring if we knew exactly what was coming around every corner? We wouldn't be excited, we wouldn't challenge ourselves, and we couldn't joyfully anticipate what we could only hope would happen.

Life is meant to be a mystery for a reason; we are meant to unfold gradually and organically according to the impulses of our soul's wisdom. If a psychic could tell us every little detail of our lives, we might momentarily be relieved to know that things will turn out all right, but the pleasure of anticipation would be sadly absent.

The task for us now is to live in the question rather than seek to stamp our lives with an answer. Perhaps our soul mate will be waiting for us tomorrow at the diner, or maybe we will run right into this person while taking our lifelong dream trek in the Himalayas. Whatever God intends for us is the great mystery we would do well to embrace.

So whatever your dream is, whatever your heart longs for, know that you will forever be discovering the great mystery of love. Enjoy the journey will all your being. And expect a miracle!

Seven Everyday Tips to Assist in Step 7, Staying the Course:

1. Keep it simple.

2. When someone criticizes you, rather than take it to heart, thank them for sharing and move on.

3. Play big and go for broke. Don't limit yourself by small vision. Permit yourself to go further than you might have imagined.

4. Complete small tasks to experience the sensation of accomplishment.

5. If something in your life is contrary to your vision, give it up and/or get rid of it.

6. When you start obsessing on details of how the relationship should unfold, go to a movie to take your mind off of it.

7. Have a party to celebrate what you know is already on the way!

Recommended Reading

Over the years I have been blessed with the insights and perspectives of many wonderful teachers. I thought you might be interested in checking out some of the books that have influenced me most.

Al-Anon. *Courage to Change* (New York: Alanon Family Group Headquarters, 1992).

Bloodworth, Venice. *Key to Yourself* (California: DeVorss and Company, 1952).

Capra, Fritjof. *The Tao of Physics* (New York: Bantam/Shambhala, 1975).

Dalai Lama. *Ethics for the New Millennium* (New York: Riverhead Books, 2001).

Foundation for Inner Peace. *A Course in Miracles* (California: Foundation for Inner Peace, 1975).

Gibran, Kahlil. *The Prophet* (New York: Random House, 1976).

Hesse, Herman. *Siddhartha* (New York: Bantam, 1982).

Huffington, Arianna. *The Fourth Instinct: The Call of the Soul*

(New York: Simon & Schuster, 1994).

Lao-Tzu. *Tao Te Ching* (London: Penguin Classics, 1963).

Moore, Thomas. *Soul Mates* (New York: HarperCollins, 1994).

Murphy, Dr Joseph. *The Power of Your Subconscious Mind* (New York: Bantam/Prentice-Hall, Inc., 1963).

Paramahansa Yoganda. *Autobiography of a Yogi* (California: Self Realization Fellowship, 1946).

Sogyal Rinpoche. *The Tibetan Book of Living and Dying* (San Francisco: HarperSanFrancisco, 1992).

Thich Nhat Hanh. *Teachings on Love* (Berkeley, CA: Parallax Press, 1998).

Tolle, Eckhart. *The Power of Now* (Novato, CA: New World Library, 1999).

Williamson, Marianne. *A Return to Love* (New York: HarperCollins, 1996).

Zukav, Gary. *The Dancing Wu Li Masters* (New York: Bantam, 1994).

Ordering and Contact Information

I have created five CDs, each one containing a twenty-minute guided meditation on a specific area of growth and change. The topics are:

1. Finding a Great Relationship

2. Perfect Weight

3. Abundance

4. Healing

5. The Daily Dose

My CDs are available from Music Design (1-800-862-7232 toll-free within the U.S., or 1-414-961-8380 outside the U.S.) or you can go to my website at www.kathyfreston.com and find ordering information there. Please also check my website for updates and special features as well.

A former actress and Ford model, Kathy Freston is a meditation counselor who conducts popular workshops in New York and Los Angeles. Her CDs offering guidance meditation have been featured in *W*, *Self*, *Fitness* and *Mode*. She and her husband divide their time between New York and Los Angeles.

SETTING YOUR HEART ON FIRE
Seven Invitations to Liberate Your Life
by Raphael Cushnir

Setting Your Heart on Fire is a wake-up call from your own heart, and a roadmap to the kind of love that most of us have rarely tasted. This is a love of awesome power – a dynamic, primal force that holds the key to your deepest and most lasting fulfilment.

Raphael Cushnir's own experiences have taught him that life's challenges, losses and disappointments can shut us down and leave us feeling empty and alone. In *Setting Your Heart on Fire* he offers an invigorating way to reawaken both your heart and your spirit. Here, through seven inspiring and easy-to-grasp Invitations, each one a building block to a new future, he reveals how you can:

- courageously and confidently reassess your choices
- let go of harmful habits, behaviours and beliefs
- heal deeply rooted emotional wounds
- revolutionize your approach to stress and adversity
- struggle less and achieve more
- open yourself to love's creativity and wisdom
- infuse everyday experiences with a breathtaking sense of joy and wonder

Accepting the Seven Invitations will enable you to blaze through any obstacle you may face and unlock the door to a fearless, authentic life. Your relationships – with family, friends, colleagues and romantic partners – will become a vehicle for profound and thrilling change. For when your heart is on fire, its light transforms the whole world.

'An enticing invitation to awaken to love'
Tara Bennett-Goleman, author of *Emotional Alchemy*

'A practical manual for the heart, a powerful invitation to live with love as the guiding force in all our relationships'
Sharon Salzberg, author of *Lovingkindness*

A Bantam Paperback

0 553 81547 4

THERE MUST BE MORE THAN THIS
How to Find More Life, Love and Meaning by Overcoming Your
Soft Addictions – Seemingly Harmless, Time-wasting Habits
by Judith Wright

'A timely book that reminds us that the physical, emotional and
spiritual nourishment we seek can be ours once we begin to let go
of habitual behaviours'
Deepak Chopra, author of *The Seven Spiritual Laws of Success*

We all want to lead fulfilling and purposeful lives. But too often
we are trapped by our seemingly harmless dependence on 'soft
addictions' – time-wasting habits such as shopping, watching TV,
gossiping and surfing the Net – which distract us and insulate us
from our thoughts, our feelings and from other people. These
habitual behaviours may provide a superficial high that satisfy our
surface needs, but they also – more alarmingly – form a powerful
net that prevents us from achieving our goals, our ambitions, and
our dreams.

In *There Must Be More Than This*, Judith Wright draws upon her
vast experience in the world of personal and professional
development to provide a unique and completely practical
eight-step programme that will help you to abandon the trivial
routines that fill your day and shows you how to focus on what
really matters. As you follow this inspiring programme, your
'soft addictions' will begin to fall away and you will develop a
deeper and more meaningful way of life – a life of true purpose,
creativity and love.

'A wise and perceptive book . . . Read it and use it and realize its
truth for yourself'
Andrew Harvey, author of *Sun and Midnight*

A Bantam Paperback

0 553 81590 3

EVERYDAY GRACE
Having Hope, Finding Forgiveness and Making Miracles
by Marianne Williamson

What do your spiritual convictions have to do with traffic jams, job anxiety, reading the newspaper, or arguing with your spouse? Everything, according to Marianne Williamson, for it is the way we live in our everyday world that determines and shapes who we are. So, Buddhist or Muslim, Christian or Jew, it is the moment when your daughter fails her exam, when your best friend lands *your* dream job, or your business instinct tells you to watch your back, that tests and builds your living faith.

In *Everyday Grace*, Marianne Williamson teaches us to ride the currents of our everyday ups and downs and shows us how to find, in each moment, an opening to the soul. For the soul is a storehouse of spiritual riches and mystical powers, and as she helps us mine our inner resources, she lays the foundation for a more graceful life. It is a life free of blame and judgement, a life in which how we get there is as important as where we're going – a life in which miracles can happen.

Once we harness the mystical power within us, we can change ourselves, our lives, and our world. We can begin to see the miracles going on all around us – and begin to work the magic of miracles ourselves.

So close your eyes, take a deep breath, open this book, and let the magic begin.

A Bantam Paperback

0 553 81545 8

THE ART OF EFFORTLESS LIVING
Simple Techniques for Healing Mind, Body and Spirit
by Ingrid Bacci Ph.D.

'A profound and potent guide to making transformative shifts in
body, mind and spirit'
Jean Houston, Ph.D., author of *The Search for the Beloved*

Most of us believe that in order to achieve anything worthwhile,
whether in our careers, family life, health or even on the sports
field, we have to work hard and apply a lot of effort. In fact, just
the opposite is true. In *The Art of Effortless Living*, Dr Ingrid Bacci
offers compelling evidence that the most productive, creative and
healthiest individuals are those who practice effortless living. By
doing less, paradoxical as it may seem, they achieve more.

Here, as you learn how to dissolve conscious and unconscious
stress through simple techniques that replace effort with
effortlessness, you will discover a more rewarding lifestyle that
leads to physical vitality, increased productivity, creative
relationships and the freedom to express your best self.

'This book contains a piece of essential wisdom – that by letting
go we gain more, not less. Because most of us are obsessed with
the idea of making things happen, we seriously need the lessons
of *The Art of Effortless Living*'
Larry Dossey, M.D., author of *Recovering Your Soul*

A Bantam Paperback

0 553 81440 0

A SELECTED LIST OF NON-FICTION TITLES
AVAILABLE FROM BANTAM BOOKS

81440 0	THE ART OF EFFORTLESS LIVING	Ingrid Bacci	£7.99
50662 5	SIMPLE ABUNDANCE	Sarah Ban Breathnach	£12.99
81260 2	SOMETHING MORE	Sarah Ban Breathnach	£12.99
81354 4	THE BOOK OF ANSWERS	Carol Bolt	£9.99
81487 7	THE BOOK OF LOVE ANSWERS	Carol Bolt	£9.99
34539 7	HANDS OF LIGHT	Barbara Ann Brennan	£19.99
34556 6	LIGHT EMERGING	Barbara Ann Brennan	£19.99
81547 4	SETTING YOUR HEART ON FIRE	Raphael Cushnir	£7.99
81564 4	A TRAVEL GUIDE TO HEAVEN	Anthony Destefano	£7.99
81323 4	THE JOURNEY TO YOU	Ross Heaven	£7.99
81496 6	ZEN AND THE ART OF FALLING IN LOVE	Charlotte Kasl	£6.99
50544 0	THE WHEEL OF LIFE	Elisabeth Kubler-Ross	£8.99
81527 X	THE SOUL'S RELIGION	Thomas Moore	£7.99
81526 1	THE SOUL OF SEX	Thomas Moore	£7.99
50527 0	ANATOMY OF THE SPIRIT	Caroline Myss	£8.99
71301 3	TAKE TIME FOR YOUR LIFE	Cheryl Richardson	£7.99
81371 4	LIFE MAKEOVERS	Cheryl Richardson	£7.99
81449 4	STAND UP FOR YOUR LIFE	Cheryl Richardson	£7.99
81380 3	SHAMAN, HEALER, SAGE	Alberto Villoldo	£7.99
81545 8	EVERYDAY GRACE	Marianne Williamson	£9.99
81590 3	THERE MUST BE MORE THAN THIS	Judith Wright	£7.99